F or five years
Tito had held his secret shame
inside. It simmered within him.
He was a pressure cooker,
blowing off steam at the
slightest provocation. Every
insult was a threat to his
manhood. His very personhood
was always at issue. The
fighting, the stealing, the back
talk had all been desperate
attempts to say, "I matter!"

It would be nice to be able
to say that Tito's problems were
solved when he raised his hand
at that ICI meeting and became
a Christian. Christ does change
people's lives, and he changed
Tito's—but not overnight. Tito
entered God's kingdom as a
troubled, self-hating brawler. It
would take some work to mold
him into Christ's image.

Child of the City

TITO MATIAS

with

RANDY PETERSEN

LIVING BOOKS®
Tyndale House Publishers, Inc.
Wheaton, Illinois

Front cover illustration © 1989 by Rick Johnson

While the people and events in this story are real,
some names have been changed to protect some
persons and their families.

Living Books is a registered trademark of Tyndale
House Publishers, Inc.

Library of Congress Catalog Card Number 89-51047
ISBN 0-8423-7224-5
Copyright © 1989 by Inner City Impact
All rights reserved
Printed in the United States of America

3   4   5   6   7   8   9   94   93   92

To those
committed urban missionaries
that make up the staff of
Inner City Impact

Contents

ONE
Child of the City 9

TWO
Community in Crisis 15

THREE
Little Men 19

FOUR
Independence Day 25

FIVE
Gang Warfare 31

SIX
Winter Games 41

SEVEN
Miracle on North Avenue 49

EIGHT
Crossing the Line 61

NINE
Special Delivery 71

TEN
Only a Game 75

ELEVEN
The Olympics 81

TWELVE
"Bonehead" Makes Good *101*

THIRTEEN
A Secret Storm *107*

FOURTEEN
The Road Back *117*

FIFTEEN
Buck Rogers Goes to High School *121*

SIXTEEN
Blessed Are Those Who Mourn *129*

SEVENTEEN
Getting Out *139*

EIGHTEEN
Home on the Range *149*

NINETEEN
Montana Miracles *159*

TWENTY
Commencement Activities *165*

TWENTY-ONE
When God Calls *175*

TWENTY-TWO
Tito's Epilogue *181*

TWENTY-THREE
When a Culture Consumes Its Young *187*

TWENTY-FOUR
The Challenge *195*

1. Child of the City

"Ugly! Ugly!" the children shouted. Young Tito felt the anger swelling inside. "Ug-ly! Ug-ly!" It was a chant now, just syllables aimed like darts at the little kid with the big head. "Ug-ly! Ug-ly!" The children cackled with delight at their baiting game. Tomorrow they might pick on someone else, taunt another, get another reaction. Today Tito was the target, and for him it was no game. Those verbal darts struck him deep.

He knew he'd be a fool to fight back. He was outnumbered. If only Luis, his little brother, were there. Luis and Tito would take on anyone, but by himself Tito would just look dumb and get hurt, provoking more taunts. So he ran.

His feet flew over the cracked Chicago sidewalks, across the street, down the alley. For a moment, the joy of running helped him forget the reason for his flight. The adrenaline exploded through his arteries as he felt the sun hot on his face and the wind cool, the sharp aliveness of his knees and ankles. His eyes took in the barrage of images: shop after shop, each with its colored sign and bilingual promises; the parked cars, some flashy, some stripped; the dumpsters; the hydrants; the scrawlings on the walls.

But then the surge subsided. Adrenaline was replaced by self-doubt. Tito's mind caught up with his body, and he heard the taunts again. "Ug-ly! Ug-ly!" His feet beat a rhythm against the cruel pavement. "Ug-ly! Ug-ly!" Each step reminded him that he couldn't run away from himself.

He turned the corner onto North Campbell and raced to his house. He hurried past his sisters playing on the living room floor, up to his room on the third story. The little kid with the big head stood in front of his mirror and quietly cried.

Tito was born with water on the brain, which caused no permanent damage but left him with an abnormally large head. He knew his body would eventually grow to match it, but meanwhile he was out of proportion, something his schoolmates never let him forget.

But his body was doing just fine. Tito could outrun just about anybody at school. He was clumsy at times, yet he excelled at sports. In baseball, Tito would often be picked before older kids. At age seven or eight, Tito had reason to be proud of what his body could do, but he was ashamed of his oddness.

He was in progress, under construction, slowly becoming normal. Someday he would be in proportion, but as he gazed into his looking-glass, Tito feared that day would never come.

Tito shared the third floor of the house with his grandmother, a devout woman with much love and many rules. Tito's two sisters had to stay inside after school—the family believed girls belonged at home—but Ricky, Tito, and Luis would roam freely through the neighborhood. Grandmother insisted that the boys wear their hair short, that they wear shirts to the dinner table, and that they pray before going to bed. Each night she would kneel with Tito and recite a prayer that Tito would repeat line by line. "Thank you for this day. Please bless Mom. Please bless Dad. Bless my brothers and sisters, Help me be a good boy."

Very early, Tito had shown a deep love for his grandmother—more than his brothers and sisters had. When he was two, Grandmother moved back to Puerto Rico for a time. Tito made such a fuss that, when she returned, his parents let him live up on the third floor with her. He grew up living by her rules at home, by his own rules on the street. When he got into trouble, he would pray that Grandmother wouldn't find out. He didn't want to hurt her. Luis didn't care; he'd pick a fight right in front of the house. But Tito tried to do his misbehaving far from home.

The two boys often played together. Just a year apart, they looked somewhat alike. Even with Tito's oversized head, they had similar features. Throughout his life, this would cause problems for Tito. Luis was a little bit quicker, but Tito was bolder. They would throw stones at passing cars, and, when one stopped, Luis would run while Tito stood his ground. They agreed that there were times to run and times to fight, but they didn't always agree on which times were which. Sometimes Tito would square around to fight, then turn to see Luis, not right behind him but a block away and moving fast. When they got their signals straight, however, they were a dynamic duo—Batman and Robin of the schoolyard and side streets.

Their neighborhood, the Humboldt Park area of Chicago's northwest side, was their playground, a place where imagination did wonders with only a few props. A rubber ball could turn a brick wall into a stadium. A few coins pitched against a curb could be the World Series. Today Tito might be the strike-out artist Ferguson Jenkins, winding up to hurl against Pete Rose. Tomorrow he'd be batting champ Bill Madlock, stroking a game-winning single off Steve Carlton.

The Moos School, where Tito spent his grade-school years, may not have taught him much, but it offered some great surfaces to run and play on. The building, a four-story hunk of deep red stone, looked like some many-eyed monster swallowing up the children of the community. But each afternoon it would spew them out again. Boys and girls would stream out of its doors, free at last. Soon they would be throwing rubber balls at the stone walls, as if teasing the beast.

This was the school where Tito's third grade teacher loved to call him "Bonehead." Tito himself assumed he was stupid, so why try? He lived for afternoons and weekends—and those fun-packed summers.

2. Community in Crisis

Humboldt Park had long been used as a stepping-stone into American society. At the turn of the century it was home to German and Swedish immigrants. Then Poles, Ukrainians, and other Europeans moved in. These all stopped—sometimes for a generation or two—in Humboldt Park before moving on to better sections of the city or out to the suburbs. It was an Ellis Island of sorts, only the experience was stretched out over a few decades. Immigrants would learn the language, study the styles, and start climbing the socioeconomic ladder.

In the 1950s a wave of migration from Puerto Rico began. The island was facing economic difficulties. Thousands set out for the brighter promises of the mainland, settling in New York, Chicago, Milwaukee, and elsewhere. Puerto Rico is a U.S. territory, so the move was easy—no passports or visas required.

Tito's father, Gilberto Matias, came to Chicago in 1954, along with his father. They both worked in a factory at first. Tito's grandfather began selling snow cones in the summertime, eventually amassing enough profit to buy a house.

Gilberto began to sell insurance, doing quite well at it. He returned to Puerto Rico to get married and brought his bride back to Chicago in 1960. Shortly afterward, Maria Cristina bore their first child, Ricky. Then followed a daughter, Abby, a few years later. Then, in quick succession, two sons, Tito and Luis, and a daughter, Nancy. Tito was born in 1966, the year of the riot.

1966. The streets of Humboldt Park burned hot that summer. Anger, fear, and frustration simmered just below the boiling point. Longtime white residents felt their community becoming Hispanic. While some lived peaceably with their Puerto Rican neighbors, remembering that they themselves (or their parents or grandparents) were once newcomers, others resented the invasion.

The Puerto Rican population seemed to expand daily. A family would send one or two members over from the mainland, and, when they were established, brothers and sisters and cousins would join them. A building that housed two might suddenly hold ten, then fifteen.

There was suspicion and misunderstanding. Why

didn't these people learn to speak English? And what sort of mischief were they plotting as they spoke to each other in their rapid patter?

The police compounded the problems. This was before "police brutality" became a nationwide no-no. In the 1950s and 1960s Chicago cops had a reputation for dealing with anything suspicious by arresting it, beating it, or shooting it. And all Puerto Ricans were perceived as suspicious.

There were reports of Humboldt Park residents being arrested for standing in front of their houses. Not dealing drugs. Not bearing weapons. Not even talking loud. Just standing. One Puerto Rican man said he was hauled to the station and beaten freely by many passing policemen before being released, uncharged. Police would become annoyed at those who would not answer them in English or those who, when asked their name, would rattle off three or four names. Having several names was and is common practice in Hispanic cultures, but police thought they were being mocked. "Better drag this wise guy to the station and teach him a lesson"—that was the standard reaction to the "invasion" from Puerto Rico.

The system was not working for Puerto Ricans in Chicago. It worked against them. The white immigrants from Europe had already stepped from Humboldt Park into the mainstream of American society. By working hard, they advanced to better housing, better schools, better jobs. But Puerto Ricans ran into racial barriers. Because of their skin color and their language, doors were closed to them. Humboldt Park was now no stepping-stone. It became a dead-end street.

In the summer of 1966, Humboldt Park was looking at itself in a mirror and crying. *When will Puerto Ricans grow into society? When will they catch up? Will they ever be normal citizens?*

June 12, 1966. The intersection of Division and Damen. A policeman shoots and kills Arturo Cruz, a twenty-one-year-old Puerto Rican. An angry crowd gathers. Police try to disperse them, bringing in vicious dogs. One person is bitten. The tension erupts into violence. For three days, Puerto Ricans march in the streets, looting and burning shops, especially those owned by whites. Police and community leaders plead for an end to the violence. It runs its course. Three days of rioting, then the community picks up the pieces. Final totals: sixteen injured, no one killed; forty-nine arrested; fifty shops vandalized; thousands of dollars in damage. The newspapers decry the violence but call for more attention to the Puerto Rican plight.

3. Little Men

As a child, Tito knew little about racial prejudice. Children are amazingly color-blind. Tito played with blacks and whites, Puerto Ricans and Mexicans. They made fun of his looks, but not his race.

In 1968 the Matias family bought a house on North Campbell, in a section of Humboldt Park that was still largely European. They were the first Puerto Rican family on the block, and they got along well with their neighbors.

This became Tito's turf. He and Luis grew up there, memorizing the cracks on the sidewalk, counting the steps to the corner. Dad's insurance business was going well. Mom stayed home and worked hard to keep her five children clean and well-fed. They were beginning to make it work. They were climbing the ladder, realizing the American Dream.

In Hispanic cultures, as in many others, women stay home. They rule the roost while their men fly free. Men strut their stuff on the street. They fight, drink, gamble, and fool around with other women. Then they come back to a home that can't contain them. Home is the province of women and children. Men don't really belong there.

Tito's father spent more and more time away from home. He was gambling. In 1972 he had to sell the house to pay a betting debt. The family continued to live in the home, paying rent. The ladder of success had broken beneath him. The American Dream was still just a dream.

The Matias boys learned machismo from their father and other men of their clan. They developed that Latin male style. They cultivated the tough talk, the dare, the thrust-out chest, the put-up fists. They exuded an air of confidence—even if they were shaking inside. They learned to hide their hurts. They learned that a macho man does not say, "I love you."

As Tito grew, he stopped running away from the taunting. He began to fight back. Luis and Tito made a formidable pair. They were cocky, running wild through the neighborhood, learning what they could get away with.

One day they went down to the school to play pinners. The game involved throwing a ball against the building. Certain alcoves of the school were perfect for it. But when Tito and Luis arrived, all the alcoves were taken.

No problem. Luis interrupted one of the games, grabbed the ball, and threw it on the roof. Without a ball, the other kids couldn't play anymore. They were mad, but they wouldn't dare challenge Luis and Tito. The Matias boys produced their own ball and began slinging it against the bricks as the previous occupants shuffled away.

Sometimes Tito would throw a sack over his shoulder and head to Woolworth's or Walgreen's with Luis at his side. There they would fill the bag with stuff they wanted—sweat socks with pictures of Superman or the Incredible Hulk. Hot Rod toy cars. Other guys had stuff like this, so Tito and Luis should have it too. The boys would run out of the store, down the alley, and unpack their loot, gloating over the ease of their heist.

At the Pentecostal church, where Mom and Grandmother would faithfully drag their children, Tito added sleight-of-hand to his other skills. Grown-ups would ask young Tito to take their offering envelopes up to the collection plate. The offering procession was part of the church's ritual, but some of the older folks would rather not make the trek, so they let the kids do it for them. Tito would stop to tie his shoe, slip the envelope into his sock, and fake putting it into the plate.

At the time, Tito's class at school was collecting for charity. Kids would bring in their dimes and quarters to help the victims of some dread disease. Tito showed up with twenty-dollar bills—the money he had taken from the offering envelopes. He wanted his classmates to think well of him. In a twisted Robin Hood scenario, Tito had stolen from the church to give to a charity.

His teacher thought it odd that a kid from a struggling family would be so generous. He called Tito's father: Was any money missing from home? The answer was a puzzled no.

"Where did you get that money?" Tito's father demanded. Tito figured he was about to get hit. Dad had that look in his eye. *Think fast*.

"I found it!" Tito stammered. "This gang member stole a lady's purse and then he saw the cops coming so he dropped it on the street and that's where I found it. I didn't know what to do with it 'cause if I gave it to the cops they'd think I stole it, and if I left it there someone else would steal it, so I took the money. But I couldn't keep it—that would be wrong. So I gave it to the charity at school."

Clever. Tito's father didn't really believe it, but it was elaborate enough to forestall a spanking. Tito had artfully dodged punishment, something he would learn to do well.

Not that Tito never got spanked. He did. By Mom and Dad. By Grandmother. By Uncle Fabian. His upbringing was shared by the whole family, it seemed, and since he was always misbehaving, he was always being swatted by someone. He wasn't always sure what he was being punished for. He was just a bad kid, and bad kids get hit—when they get caught. He longed to please his father, his friends, his teachers, and especially his grandmother. But he didn't have the faintest notion of how to do that. Somehow he found himself always doing wrong.

4. Independence Day

1977. June 4—Puerto Rican Independence Day.

A bomb exploded on the fifth floor of the Cook County Building in downtown Chicago. Since it was Saturday, no employees were hurt in the blast, but it caused six thousand dollars worth of damage. A Puerto Rican terrorist group, the FALN, claimed responsibility. Police worried about rising tensions in Chicago's Puerto Rican community.

Many residents of the Humboldt Park community spent the day in the park—the grassy square that gives the community its name. Puerto Rican Day was a grand fiesta. There was a parade, and for much of the day the park was crammed with picnickers, strollers, concessions, musicians. It was a scorching afternoon, and the revelers sought various ways to beat the heat: water ice, ice cream, soda pop, beer. A happy patter of voices rose above the strains of music that blared from different corners of the park.

As afternoon ambled into evening, some of the families packed up and went home. Young toughs strutted around the park. Alcohol was prevalent—and drugs. The happy patter turned to jeering and taunting.

Around six in the evening a gunshot ripped through the park. Then another. As the reports put it later, it was gang vs. gang. The Latin Kings, the longtime lords of this turf, were being challenged by the upstart Spanish Cobras. Police moved in to quell the violence. They only made it worse.

Julio Osorio, a twenty-six-year-old gang member who was probably drunk, saw two cops coming and fired at them. He ran to hide behind a tree and fired again. The police shot back, killing him. One of their bullets apparently hit Rafael Cruz, also a gang member, also aged twenty-six.

The crowd turned on the police, throwing bricks and bottles at them. Gangs continued to shoot at each other. Cars were being driven through the park at high speed in crazy games of chicken. Three vehicles were set on fire and pushed into the park lagoon. The police on patrol in the park were powerless to stop the chaos. Attacks on them grew so bad that a lieutenant ordered the police out of the area, apparently thinking that would cool the situation.

It didn't. Wild crowds swept onto California and Division Streets, breaking windows and looting shops. The burglar alarm at Woolworth's rang, but no one seemed to care as looters helped themselves to the merchandise. A corner bar was robbed of all its liquor. Someone set fire to the Fair Share grocery store. At White's department store, looters grabbed clothes off mannequins. Two police cars were overturned and burned.

A three-story brick building at the corner of Division and Washtenaw was gutted by fire. When firemen approached to put out the blaze, they were turned back by the rock-throwing mob. Later a man was found dead inside.

An estimated three thousand people took part in the rioting. When police reinforcements arrived, they donned riot gear. More than two hundred of them swept through the streets. Police helicopters hovered overhead, shining searchlights down upon the chaos. By midnight, the violence simmered down.

Three men had been killed, at least 116 people injured.

Residents spent Sunday sweeping up, shaking their heads, standing out on their sidewalks talking about the rioting. That evening there was another outbreak. About three hundred youths began throwing rocks and Molotov cocktails at police patrols. Another thirteen police and four civilians were injured.

When the weekend was over, police had arrested 164 people. Though they blamed gangs for the violence, only fifteen of those arrested were minors.

"Clearly these were not kids letting off steam," said the police superintendent. "These were adults who should have had the maturity to realize the results of their actions."

It was the worst rioting in the eleven years since the riot of 1966. Back then, you could almost understand it. *Everybody* rioted in the sixties. American minorities launched a gargantuan struggle for civil rights. But these were the "enlightened" seventies. Everyone had civil rights by now, didn't they?

Social analysts reviewed the factors that fed the frustration of Chicago's Puerto Ricans: poor housing, poor schools, lack of recreational facilities, lack of social services, police harassment, little or no voice in government. "We have brought these problems to the attention of City Hall for ten to twelve years," complained the president of the Puerto Rican Chamber of Commerce. "Fires and arsons. Youth gangs. Police harassing people. Lack of city services. And when community leaders went to see Mayor Bilandic after the riots, he kept them waiting three and a half hours and gave them twenty minutes to discuss all this."

At the time of the riots, Latinos (including Mexicans, Cubans, and other Hispanics as well as Puerto Ricans) accounted for nearly 25 percent of Chicago's population, yet they held only 1.7 percent of city government jobs. Only one police district had a Latino commander, and he was injured in the rioting. Only one school, Moos, had a Puerto Rican principal. And the city had no Latino council members, state legislators, or Congressmen.

Chicago politicians play hardball. It's a game of power and patronage. The Puerto Rican community hadn't learned those games yet—or at least they were being kept out of the contest. Their frustration, some were saying, had erupted in their own show of power, the Puerto Rican Day riots.

Whatever the reasons, the rioting gave the Puerto Rican community a black eye. "Today I am embarrassed that I am Puerto Rican," one woman told a *Chicago Tribune* reporter the day after the rioting. A man confessed, "I am Puerto Rican, but for the first time in my life yesterday I lied. I told a man who asked me, 'I am not Puerto Rican.'"

The community found itself in a downward spiral. Feeling disenfranchised, powerless, abused by society at large, some residents resorted to violence. This merely confirmed society's impressions of the Puerto Rican community—that they didn't deserve power. And it made the Puerto Ricans more sure that they would never win within the system.

In such an environment, gangs look good. A gang is a franchise, a place to be somebody, to wield power. A gang beats the system, or tries to. Chicago gangs were—are—a long way from the *West Side Story* Saturday night rumble. These weren't kids looking for something to do. These were frustrated adults lashing out against a society that refused to acknowledge them. The gangs that sparked the 1977 riots had managed to capture the support of a surprising number of disenfranchised citizens. Those riots signaled the emergence of gang power within the community.

Astute Puerto Ricans realized that the gangs caused more problems than they solved. But the gangs continued to weave themselves into the fabric of community life.

5. Gang Warfare

"They're gonna fight." That was the word on the street. Tito was only eight, but he and Luis heard the whispers. "The Latin Kings," someone said. "Maple Park." Just a block away from the boys' home.

Tito and his brother hurried to see what was happening. As they ran along North Avenue, they looked up to see guys with guns in the third-story windows—waiting. The air was crisp with the excitement of impending battle. The boys turned the corner, and there it was, Maple Park, with two or three hundred guys armed with knives, chains, bats, guns, ready for the action to begin.

Gang war was different then. Today guys drive by, roll down a car window, and shoot you on a street corner. Then it was more organized—more civilized, if you will. It was more like Napoleon's troops marching into battle, meeting another army at a des-

ignated time and place. Now it's guerrilla warfare—
shoot and run.

Tito and Luis left the park before the fight started.
It was no place for little kids. But they had caught
the scent of excitement, of violence. Their world was
no longer just one of stickball and racing each other
to the corner. Wars were being fought a block away.

This was before the 1977 riot. It was the early
1970s. The neighborhood had changed, and it kept
changing. Every day Hispanic families moved into
Humboldt Park, and not just Puerto Ricans, but
Mexicans too, and some Cubans. Gangs sprang up
among these new residents, and the various groups
vied for control of the turf.

The Latin Kings, the Latin Disciples, the Spanish
Cobras, the Insane Unknowns. These and many others were strutting the streets, showing their colors,
spraying graffiti to mark off their territory. In 1975,
police estimated that there were 147 gangs in Chicago, with memberships running from six to three
thousand in each gang. Total gang membership: at
least ten thousand.

Chicago has always had gangs. Longtime mayor
Richard J. Daley had belonged to an Irish street
gang in his youth. Immigrants from Eastern Europe
banded together for social and political reasons and
brought their national prejudices with them. World
wars were fought on Chicago's streets.

Such gangs worked within the system and without,
often running afoul of the law. Chicago's gangsters of

the 1920s and 1930s attained legendary status in their battles with federal agents. A key factor was that most of these ethnic gangs were systems unto themselves. These newcomers couldn't count on the normal social machinery of Chicago to work for them, so they built their own machines.

The 1960s saw a resurgence in gang activities in Chicago and other cities of the U.S. Blacks and Hispanics were forming gangs in the inner city and staking out their turf. There was some violence and some drug-dealing, but nowhere near the amount seen today. Gangs tended to get their money through extortion and welfare rip-offs.

A major transition occurred in the 1970s. The results exploded in the 1980s. The first change was age: gang members were getting older. In the 1960s most gang members were youths. By the time you got to be twenty-one or twenty-five, you didn't feel like hanging out with the teen toughs anymore. It was time to grow up, get a job, be a good citizen. At least that's how it had worked before.

But it wasn't easy for a minority member in a big city to get a job in the early 1970s. For blacks and Hispanics, assimilation into the greater culture wasn't happening. But they felt at home in the gangs. They might marry and have kids, but they'd stay in the gangs—and pass on their gang loyalty to their children. By the 1980s, there were second- and even third-generation gang members. Ages ranged from seven to fifty. "We've got pictures of gang members dressing their babies in gang T-shirts, toddlers holding guns and giving gang salutes," commented one Chicago cop.

Along with age went sophistication. Gangs graduated from welfare fraud to prostitution, theft, and—above all—dealing drugs. Gangs discovered there was money to be had in narcotics, lots of it. As Al Capone and company had flouted the law to distribute alcohol a half-century earlier, street gangs began to peddle their illegal substances—heroin, speed, cocaine.

"Gangs of the 1980s are more sophisticated about crime," wrote Bonita Brodt and William Recktenwald in the *Chicago Tribune*. "Age-old rumbles over machismo and turf today are punctuated with bloody gun battles over lucrative money-making ventures. Gangs have gone from shaking down businesses in the 1960s to widespread narcotics trafficking, prostitution, and burglary rings, enterprises that one law enforcement official said rake in millions of dollars in annual profits. Gangs dip into their reserves to post bond money, hire lawyers to defend their accused, pay juveniles for a job well done, and shrewdly reinvest their money in more drugs, and even real estate, to keep the cycle going."

Certain blocks of the city became drive-in "drugstores." Suburbanites as well as city-dwellers could drive by and make a transaction in seconds. One gang recently threw a beer party for the whole block to attract new drug buyers.

"Turf" came to mean more than just a place to belong; it was valuable merchandising territory.

Gangs would fight over the right to sell drugs on a particular block. With all the money available, they could wield more expensive weapons. Automatic rifles, Uzis, and machine guns made their way into the city. The major gangs were making deals with other countries for drugs and arms. By the 1980s, "rumbles" were long gone. Gang fights were bloodbaths. "There were killings in the 1960s," said the head of the Chicago police's gang crimes unit. "But gangs at that time were not as violent overall. There is more killing today over a larger area."

"It seems like they are always shooting over here," said one resident of the Cabrini-Green housing project on Chicago's Near North side. "When they start, people duck for cover like they duck from the rain. When the shooting stops, people go on about their business."

Apart from wrangling over turf and drugs, revenge is a major factor in gang violence. It's a cycle like the Greek tragedies. Somebody kills your brother, you kill him. But then his brother has to kill you, and on and on. Vengeance is a matter of honor. "The highest honor you can give for your set [gang] is death," one gang member related. "When you die, when you go out in a blaze of glory, you are respected. When you kill for your set, you earn your stripes—you put work in."

Drive-by shootings have become commonplace in Chicago and other cities. If you have an account to settle, load up your gun and drive to enemy turf. Find a rival gang member and let him have it.

Neighborhood residents—and anyone passing through the areas where gang violence is likely—must surely wish that gang members were better marksmen. "Keep in mind we don't have no target ranges . . . where we get prolific with these guns," one Los Angeles gang member told an interviewer.

"Shoot till you're out of bullets, then back up," said another.

"Bullet ain't got no name," added a third, "hit whatever it hit."

Sadly, innocent bystanders often get hit in drive-by shootings.

Prison, authorities are now admitting, is like a school for gangs. In Illinois prisons, some say, everyone has to join a gang; there's no alternative. If a young criminal is not a gang member when he is sent to jail, he will surely be one when he gets out. In the early 1980s the gangs of Chicago divided into two major groupings, People and Folks. The alliances were forged by imprisoned gang leaders, and word was sent out to their followers.

Every gang has its core leadership; its climbers, vying for position and respect within the gang; and its marginal members, who join the gang merely to avoid the consequences of not joining. In the 1970s, there were age divisions. "Peewees" started as young as seven or eight. Young kids like this are still used to run drugs—if they're caught, the courts won't do much to them. "Futures" began around age thirteen. The leaders, usually in their twenties and thirties, were already grooming the next generation.

Violence and crime are the ways into a gang. Prospective members often get "jumped in"—that is, they fight the whole gang. If they're tough enough to take a beating from everyone in the gang, they qualify for membership. For some, committing a crime can establish a place in a gang. And, as in any social club, it helps to know someone. If you have a friend in the gang, it makes it easier to join.

Once initiated, you are introduced to the codes and rituals of the gang. It's not unlike a religion. You take on a "street name." You use special words and phrases. You wear certain colors. You wear your clothing a certain way. You identify yourself with hand signals. Some even have gang prayers.

Volumes have been written on the sociology and psychology of gangs. How do they work? What makes kids join?

"The gang supplies, rightly or wrongly, that camaraderie that young men need," says Rita Fry, an assistant public defender who represented a gang member who killed three people. The guy joined the gang after his mother died.

"The streets are very attractive," says Thomas Cook, professor of psychology and urban affairs at Northwestern University in Evanston, just north of Chicago. "If your home life is bad, if the schools are bad, where else can you go? People escape if they have other alternatives more attractive than the streets—a good home life, an early job, a teacher who takes a special interest."

"There are several reasons [that kids join gangs], but peer pressure has to be the chief one," says Lt. Fred O'Reilly of the Chicago police. "There is also glamor. If you take a kid in an inner-city neighborhood, he may not have a father, or his dad works in a factory as a laborer. Along comes a gang leader with money, fancy car, and clothes. Why wouldn't he join a gang?"

"Human nature wants to be accepted," says Tee Rodgers, founder of a Los Angeles gang. "At that age—eleven to seventeen—all kids want to belong. They are un-people."

"If you look around and see people like Ernie Banks, you want to grow up and be a baseball player," says a former member of the Latin Kings. "But if all you see is gangbangers, you want to grow up to be a gang leader."

"Gangs breed where basic structures—such as the family, the schools, churches, community organizations—are weak," says Edward Pleines, head of the Chicago police's gang crimes unit.

"What's happening right now is that gangs have moved away from just intimidating to get youths to join gangs," said Robert Martin, head of the Chicago Intervention Network on ABC's "Nightline." "They're hooking into emotional youth needs. For example, a couple of weeks ago I had a thirteen-year-old, and he was saying that on the anniversary of the death of his mother, his gang went out to the gravesite, to sit with him. They got high, they reminisced. When I listened to him, what I heard the gang doing was grief support. And so I think it's just a matter of us reinvesting in those kinds of services again that will give kids an alternative. If we don't, the gangs are willing to do it."

From the early 1970s to the present day, Humboldt Park has been a major center of gang activity. At one point, there were nearly fifty gangs active in just the three neighboring communities of Logan Square, West Town, and Humboldt Park.

This was Tito's world. As he and his little brother skipped back along North Avenue, underneath the cocked rifles, away from the battle in Maple Park, what were the chances for them?

6. Winter Games

Chicago starts getting cold in October. The wind blows off Lake Michigan and rushes westward, between the skyscrapers, through the grid of city streets. With hot August memories still fresh in their minds, Chicagoans don their winter coats.

Nine-year-old Tito loved the summer. The warm weather provided plenty of opportunities to play. He was always looking for a game—softball, basketball, maybe just racing a friend down to Wabansia. But winter always came on too fast.

The last winter had dumped record amounts of snow on Chicago. That had provided some excellent snowball fights. And the side streets, unplowed, became skating rinks. Tito remembered the fun he had grabbing onto the back of a passing truck—making sure he had gloves on—and sliding on the frozen street. Water-skiing on ice! An expert fun-finder like

Tito could make the best of any season, but when the temperatures dropped really low, the options were more limited. Nobody stays outside for long when it's five below.

As the October wind brought winter's first chill barreling across North Avenue, Tito's spirits sank a little. The softball games on the playground became less frequent. Kids had to play in their sweaters and coats. Then it became just too cold to play outside.

Tito's friend Jesse discovered Inner City Impact, an evangelical ministry committed to discipleship and evangelism. An athletic black classmate, Jesse had been going to an old warehouse on North Avenue on certain evenings and weekends to play games. He tried to explain the games to Tito—lots of running and jumping, mostly, and if your team won, you got a candy bar. Jesse's team had been losing. He needed some fresh talent, so he asked Tito to come along. Tito liked games, and he loved candy bars. So he went with Jesse to the big white building.

The sign was big as life: Inner City Impact, crisp black letters on a white background climbing the side of the building. Tito had passed the place a million times but never paid it much attention. Inside the big metal doors, then through some other doors, then up the steps. Jesse saw some kids he knew and said hello. Tito had his tough-guy look. He was a bit scared, actually. He wanted these other kids to like him, but he had the feeling they wouldn't. He'd show them—in the games.

The staircase turned a couple of times, and then

they were on the third floor. Jesse dragged Tito through another set of doors and into a wide room where twenty or thirty other kids were running and jumping and laughing. They were just warming up, playing dodgeball, tossing a big rubber ball across the room.

Jesse and Tito jumped into the game, as did other newcomers. Soon there were about forty kids, all about their age or a little older. Most of them were Hispanic, though there were some blacks and a couple of white kids. Milling about, watching, keeping order in the game, were some white adults. Tito counted eight of them. They were easy to spot, tall and white in a sea of brown faces. But there was something else different about them.

Whistles blew, and the kids were quickly grouped into four teams, stationed at the four corners of the room. Tito looked down and noticed a white circle painted on the gray linoleum. There were lines extending like spokes from the center of the circle toward the four corners. These lines had various hash marks of uncertain meaning, as if this was some sort of elaborate religious ritual.

Each team included about ten kids and one or two adult leaders. Each was assigned a color: Tito's team was red. An older white man with a whistle stood in the center of the circle and explained the first game. It involved dribbling a basketball around the circle, then grabbing a bowling pin at the center of the circle. It seemed easy to Tito. When would they get to the running and jumping?

He looked again around the room. These adults—what were they doing here? They seemed to be in their early twenties, if that old. But in a way they seemed much younger than the kids. They seemed fresh, well-scrubbed, bright-eyed, innocent. Tito knew some guys in their twenties from the neighborhood, guys with glazed eyes, cold stares, lined faces. That's what the streets do to you—drugs, drinking, gang fights, watching your friends die, worrying about everything but never letting it show. Some of those guys he knew *too* well—he shivered deeply as he thought of them, then pushed the painful thought from his mind. These white folks knew none of that. Tito studied their faces. He watched them calling, laughing, encouraging. What was their game?

The older man with the whistle was bright with life, not a hint of the world-weariness Tito expected of someone that age. "Pastor Johnson" they called him. But what kind of a pastor was he? He wasn't preaching, just blowing a whistle and explaining the rules of each game. What was he doing here? As Tito watched him and the younger leaders it seemed that their only concern was that every kid have a good time. And, amazingly, the kids were. They were having a blast.

Tito got his chance to run. He flew around the circle and grabbed the bowling pin, bringing it back triumphantly to his cheering team.

"Who is this new kid?" someone asked.

"He's my friend Tito," said Jesse.

Tito savored that moment, but he didn't crack a smile. No, his confident gaze said, "Of course I won. I had it all along."

There were several other victories for Tito that night. He wasn't big, but he was fast. And he was smart. His quick reflexes kept him a step ahead of the others. And he had a desire. He played to win. The red team took home candy bars that night and again a few weeks later when Tito showed up again. After a few months of sporadic attendance, Tito became a regular. He got to know the games well and excelled at nearly all of them. The leaders kept reminding him that it was only a game, only a game. But Tito wasn't just playing a game, he was playing life. If he didn't win, he wasn't worth much.

He still couldn't figure out those white folks. What did they get out of this? Just a good feeling? They could go home to their suburban split-levels and rest in the knowledge that they had done a good deed for those poor inner-city kids. But the way they looked at him—they were so incredibly *open*. No glazed stares. It was like you could climb into their big eyes and move into their souls. Whatever motives they were hiding, they were hiding well. They didn't *look* like they were hiding anything.

Tito won more than his share of candy bars. But when he didn't win, he stole. That was a kind of winning all its own. Win within the system or beat the system, just get the candy bar any way you can.

One night Tito's team was losing badly—no awards tonight. So Tito sneaked away from the circle, hunting for the secret cache of candy bars. He jimmied the lock on the game room, where they kept most of the equipment. A temporary wall separated the game room from the leaders' offices, where the candy bars were kept, but the wall didn't reach all the way to the ceiling. Using the shelves for support, young Tito climbed over the wall and jumped down into the office. He found the candy bars on a desk, in plain view. He quickly filled his pockets and climbed back over the wall.

The red team did not win that night, but Tito begged one of the leaders, Paul Milkie, for a candy bar anyway.

"No, Tito," the leader explained. "You know the rules. You didn't win. You don't get a candy bar."

"But Jesse's on my team and he got one!"

"Jesse brought a visitor," Mr. Milkie said patiently. "If you brought a visitor, you could get one, too."

"But I want one now! Please!" Tito was relentless in his whining.

At the end of the evening, Mr. Milkie drove Tito the six blocks to his home, and Tito whined and cajoled the whole way. "Please! I did well enough to win tonight! It wasn't my fault! I'll bring a visitor next week, I promise!"

Finally, as he pulled up in front of the Matias house, Mr. Milkie had pity on the poor waif and offered him a candy bar. Tito thanked him and grabbed it like a trophy. Then he hopped out of the car and hurried up the front steps. There he turned and proudly pulled out from under his coat a handful of candy bars he had filched from the office. Mr. Milkie couldn't help but smile. This kid was so incredibly good at being bad. In fun, he raised his fist and shook it: "We'll get you for that!"

Inner City Impact wasn't just games. There were times of singing and Bible study. Tito found these parts kind of boring, but he could memorize some Bible verses to get candy bars. This was a game, too, and it grew on him as the months and years went by.

Something else grew on him: the love of those squeaky clean, naive white leaders. Whatever their reasons, they paid attention to him. They talked to him, asked about his family, about school. They praised him for his efforts in games and Bible learning. They scolded him for his misbehavior, but it was as if they knew he could be better. He felt that they liked him, even when he was bad. Tito was a somebody at ICI. He liked that. And he kept coming back.

7. Miracle on North Avenue

In Ireland, in the early 1900s, Michael Dillon became a born-again Christian. He was studying to be a priest; he read John 14:6—"I am the way, the truth, and the life. No man comes to the father but by me"—and he knew he needed a personal relationship with Jesus.

His Catholic family didn't understand his fervor. He was rejecting centuries of religious tradition. They disowned him.

Seeking his own religious freedom, Michael set off in a cattle boat for America, settling first in Chicago at Moody Bible Institute. Then, after spending time in Colorado and Nebraska, he returned to Chicago, where in 1918 he became the first superintendent of the Sunshine Gospel Mission, which he faithfully served for some twenty-five years.

The Roaring Twenties brought Chicago national

prominence. Architectural masterpieces sprang up throughout the city. It was the center of commerce for the U.S. heartland. Its factories employed thousands of European immigrants as the commodities trade bustled downtown. Of course, in those days of Prohibition, Billy Sunday preached against bad living, gangsters battled the feds on city streets, and organizations like the Salvation Army, YMCA, and Pacific Garden Mission sought to rescue the perishing. In the heart of the city—604 North Clark—the Sunshine Gospel Mission provided spiritual and material comforts to needy Chicagoans.

Michael's son William followed in his father's footsteps, directing the mission for twenty-seven years. The mission established a radio outreach as well. In fact, the chorus "Safe Am I" was written by William and Mildred Dillon and popularized on the broadcast.

Their son Bill wanted to be an airline executive. This was no rebellion against the family business; he just loved planes. He planned to get a business degree, get some experience with an airline, and soar to the top.

His parents suggested that he take a year of Bible education at Moody Bible Institute. That was fine: a Christian business executive should have some serious grounding in God's Word, Bill figured. He liked that one year so much, he stretched it to three. But then he resumed his plans. Finding odd jobs at O'Hare Airport during summers, Bill attended suburban Elmhurst College for business and Murray

State for an MBA to go along with his Bachelor of Theology from Moody. He was ready. Unfortunately, the industry wasn't.

Jobs in airline management were tight at the time. One by one, doors closed for Bill. He sought other jobs in business, unsuccessfully. Discouraged, he sought out a trusted Moody professor, Dr. Harold Garner.

Setting himself down in Dr. Garner's office, Bill poured out his heart. His carefully woven plans were unraveling. The corporate world was a brick wall to him. What was God doing? What did the Lord have in mind for young Bill Dillon?

The professor smiled sympathetically. "You've shared your family's burden for inner-city work all your life. Maybe your present difficulty in finding a job is really just a gentle push in that direction."

"But how—"

"I know of a church on the West Side that needs a youth pastor. It could be tough work. You know how city kids are. But if you're interested, I'll put in a good word for you."

Dr. Garner scribbled a name and number on a piece of paper and handed it to Bill. "Pray about it," he said.

Bill took the number, applied for the position, and got it. He worked with the young people of Salem Evangelical Free Church at California and Armitage. It was rigorous work, but he loved it. He loved the kids. And he built a thriving youth ministry there. But after two-and-a-half years, it was time to move on. The church was struggling and couldn't afford to pay Bill anymore. He and his wife, Sandy, began to look for other work.

It was Irving Johnson who got them thinking about Humboldt Park. About fifty years old, "Pastor" Johnson was actually the custodian at Salem Church. But he had a strong desire to help young people. He had thrilled to see Bill develop the youth group at Salem, and he was aware of the Dillons' desire to move on.

"Come on," he told Bill one day. "Let me take you for a ride." They drove down California Avenue to Humboldt Park, past the once stately houses of a bygone era, past the bilingual signs on North Avenue shops, past the huge Von Humboldt Elementary School.

"There are nine schools in a space about ten blocks square," Pastor Johnson said. "I figured it out once. About ten thousand kids."

Bill was getting the picture. "I've read about the gangs here."

"Yep. And there's a new one every day," Johnson said. "Look at the graffiti there: 'The All Mighty Maniac Latin Disciples.' They're all getting pretty powerful. It's hard for kids to say no."

"Disciples," Bill repeated. "Could we ever turn them into *real* disciples?"

They rode past the park, a playground, a church. "What about the churches here?" Bill asked.

"There are some," Johnson answered. "But they need all the help they can get. It's a changing neighborhood. Mostly Puerto Rican now. The older churches can't keep up. And there are lots of kids."

"Ten thousand of them," Bill muttered, gazing out the window.

In the summer of 1972, Bill and Sandy Dillon established Inner City Impact. The original idea was small and simple: start block clubs in Humboldt Park, clubs that kids could identify with. Gangs promised kids so much—identity, action, a sense of belonging. A Christian club could do the same thing.

Something like this doesn't happen overnight. You have to get to know kids, earn their trust. It took a lot of "hanging around" that summer, pounding the pavement, making friends. To pay the bills, Bill went door to door selling pots and pans. In late July they launched the clubs with a five-week series. They'd set up shop on a sidewalk somewhere, or in a park. They'd play some games, sing some songs, teach some Bible verses. Once a week for five weeks, until the end of summer, kids would come to the ICI club meetings. Soon the Dillons were running twelve such clubs in different blocks of the community.

With fall approaching, they needed some indoor facilities. Fortunately, they arranged to use the second floor of a Union Hall, Riggers Local 136, rent-free.

Soon, ICI adopted the Awana program. Awana had started at Chicago's Northside Gospel Center and was spreading rapidly through the nation. It was sort of a Christian version of Scouting, but games were its main claim to fame. The Awana architects had invented and collected a series of team games to be played around a circle. These were games of speed, strategy, agility, and just plain effort. Kids loved them.

The games were the magnet, attracting kids to the clubs, but the real substance was the biblical training. Kids would sing, pray, memorize verses, and hear Scripture lessons. By winning games and memorizing verses, kids would earn points toward medals or, in some clubs, more immediate gratification—such as candy bars.

Awana required adult leadership, lots of it. The one-to-one interaction of the kids with their leaders was probably the most beneficial aspect of the program. The Dillons needed to find others just as burdened for inner-city kids as they were. They began to gather volunteers from churches in the greater Chicago area and from Moody Bible Institute. Bill's winning smile and earnest dedication convinced many to give up an evening a week, or an afternoon, to work with needy kids.

The union hall was a perfect site. It was spacious enough for the Awana games, and it was right in the center of this youth-packed neighborhood: nine schools within a five-block radius. This was where the kids were.

At first the union officials allowed ICI to use the building one night a week for four weeks, rent-free.

Then it was three nights. With ICI's clubs expanding, they eventually needed access to the building every night of the week. This was granted, still free of charge.

Then Bill had a brainstorm. Why couldn't the union give the building to ICI? The ministry would lease the office space back to the union at no cost, and ICI's nonprofit status would get the building off the tax rolls. It would give ICI the kind of permanent residence in the neighborhood it needed. People had seen too many outfits come and go: Rent some space, drop a few good deeds on the locals, skip town when it gets tough. Inner City Impact had to let the community know that it was here to stay.

Bill and an associate took the union boss to lunch to spring the idea. He was willing to sell, the man said, but they'd need some money. Unfortunately, money was a commodity ICI didn't have.

The ICI board began looking for other buildings in the neighborhood, but with no substantial cash to put down, deals were hard to find. For one building, a block away from the union hall, they would need a $10,000 down payment. They began praying for this amount—$10,000 by December 25, 1973. That deal fell through, but the staff kept praying. Whatever building they would buy, they would need $10,000.

On December 21, Bill Dillon got a phone call. "Get down to the union hall right away," the voice said. "There's a fire." He hurried to the scene. North Avenue was full of fire trucks, lit up by flashing lights and the blaze from the union hall. Bill stepped over the fire hoses to get a closer look. The second floor—their recreation area—was badly damaged. What would they do?

Most of their equipment was destroyed. Even their Bibles were burned. They would need a new place to meet. Now more than ever they needed their own building. With four days remaining on their arbitrary deadline, they kept praying for $10,000.

A winter retreat was scheduled for a few days later. ICI had made a commitment to the kids, so the buses loaded up beside the burned-out building and carried the troops to Wisconsin. But would there even be an ICI when they returned? Was this Christmas retreat a last gasp for the ministry? On the bus, Bill tossed the question around in his head. Maybe it was time to quit. How could they possibly continue with no money, no meeting place, no equipment?

He thought about the call he had made to his friend Bob Murfin. The pastor of Bethel Community Church and a popular radio speaker, Murfin was brimming with wisdom. Bill had often sought his advice in tough times. And this was a tough time.

"Bill," Murfin had told him, "the pages of church history are full of stories of ministries that were raised up literally from the ashes. Sometimes God has to tear us down before he can build us up."

The kids on the bus were charged up, talking about the fire more than about the fun awaiting them in Wisconsin. Bill tried to shut out the din and concentrate on his own thoughts. Was this fire God's way of starting over? Or was he telling Bill and Sandy to head back to airline management? Had Bill been wrong to head into inner-city ministry? Doubts and worries raged through his thinking. Trying to put them aside, he quietly prayed, "Lord, it's up to you. Whatever this ministry is or isn't, it's yours. Your will be done."

On December 27, in Wisconsin, Bill got a phone call from Chicago. One staff person had stayed behind to open the mail and answer the phone. She was on the line.

"Bill, you won't believe what came in the mail today. A check for $10,000."

He was stunned. "Praise the Lord!" he said quietly.

"Of course it didn't arrive by December 25," she teased. "Maybe I should send it back."

"Don't you dare!" Bill said, laughing. "I blame the post office for the delay, not God. Who sent it?"

She read him the name on the check. He didn't recognize it.

Through directory assistance, Bill got the number of the man who had sent the check. "Hello," he said. "My name is Bill Dillon. We've never met before. But I want to thank you for the check you sent to ICI. It was a direct answer to prayer. We had been praying to receive $10,000 by Christmas. And the need was even more urgent after the fire last week. But of course you have heard about the fire."

"No," the man said. "What fire?"

ICI took up temporary residence in an Alliance church in the area. Then Bill noticed a For Sale sign on a building across from the union hall. Along with his father and another board member, Bill met with the owner, a man named Steinberg.

Steinberg wanted $100,000. They talked him down to $85,000.

"How much will you put down?" Steinberg asked.

"Ten thousand," Bill answered.

"Fine," said the owner. "And what financial institution will you go through to get the remaining seventy-five?"

"Well," Bill stammered. "We were hoping we could arrange a payment plan with you."

"You want me to carry your mortgage?" Steinberg laughed. "I really wish you'd go through a bank."

"Look, sir," Bill began, "we have a ministry here that is reaching kids. We are grabbing them before they get into gangs, and we're establishing them in good, wholesome patterns of behavior. We're keeping them off the streets.

"Now this ministry has grown like crazy in the last year-and-a-half. We have a couple dozen volunteers who give up their time to be a part of this. And we have a growing number of people and churches that are willing to give money to support our work.

"But you know as well as I do that if I go to First National Bank and say, 'Here's my idea. Lend me seventy-five grand,' they're liable to lock me up. On paper, we have nothing to stand on. But we have dedication. We are going to make this work. We're going to make sure you get your money. And the very reason we want to buy a building is that we plan to continue this ministry for a long time.

"So we're asking you: Take a chance on us. You won't be sorry."

Steinberg looked Bill square in the eye for several seconds. "I like what I hear. What sort of terms would you like?"

They arranged a ten-year mortgage at 8.25 percent interest. Shortly afterward, ICI moved into the building at 2704 W. North, which still serves as its headquarters. Thirty-five full-time "missionaries" and numerous part-timers and volunteers now work with ICI, getting to know kids, running club meetings. Many more are sought.

After thirteen years of dreaming about a multi-centered ministry, ICI branched out to the nearby community of Logan Square. They bought an old movie theater and renovated it into an activity center. Now a church that has its roots in ICI is meeting in that building. The ministry has also expanded to include the Chicago Gospel Mission in the Henry Horner Homes area on Chicago's Near West side. The leaders envision eventual expansion to other cities of the U.S. God has used 2704 W. North Avenue as a beachhead for a thriving ministry of life-style evangelism, discipleship, and church planting.

And all because of a church custodian, pots and pans, a fire, a timely check, a man named Steinberg—and the amazing power of God.

8. Crossing the Line

Every Thursday night at six Tito showed up at ICI for an evening of fun and games. He looked forward to it so much that his grandmother would threaten to keep him home from ICI if he misbehaved.

Tito's family wasn't sure what to make of ICI. It kept Tito off the streets for a few hours at least. And the kids did memorize Bible verses, so it couldn't be too bad. ICI even threw a Thanksgiving banquet for kids' families. That's where Tito's family met Bill Dillon.

Bill already had his eye on Tito. He couldn't help but marvel at Tito's command of the games he played. The kid's intensity infected others. He wanted to win, and he made sure everyone else shared that desire.

Watch enough of these games and you can pick out the winners and the losers, the leaders and the followers, the ones who will stay with you and the ones who will drop out. Bill saw a spark in Tito. Something was driving him. And he was driving everyone else.

Tito was a thermostat, setting the temperature for the group. If he was serious about a game, the others were too. But if there was trouble, you could be pretty sure Tito was at the center of it. He had a good sense of humor; he enjoyed playing pranks. But he also had a mean streak of rebellion in him. He didn't like being told what to do.

It was easy enough to harness Tito's energy during game time. He had even been pretty good at memorizing verses. But when it was time to gather the troops and sit them down for some singing and a message from the Bible, Tito could easily sabotage the whole thing. Generally, Tito and a few friends would sit up front or in back and crack jokes, distracting everyone. Bill hoped the message was getting through, but he wasn't always sure.

One evening Bill invited a special speaker to talk to the kids. This was not uncommon. Sometimes the kids took an outsider more seriously than one of the regular leaders. It might be a youth pastor from an area church or a student from Moody Bible Institute. The kids especially enjoyed Don Rackett and his sassy black puppet. Sometimes Tito and the others sat in rapt attention; other times they were terrors.

On this occasion—Tito had been attending for a couple of years now—the speaker spoke simply about the need to be saved. "We are all sinners," he said. "We have all done bad things."

A few of the kids stole glances at Tito, but he was hanging on every word.

The speaker made it so plain. "Why do we do bad things? Because there's a badness inside of us. It's like a stain you can't get out. It's worse than ring-around-the-collar."

Some kids giggled at this; Tito was transfixed.

"It really is," the speaker continued. "You try soaking it out, you try scrubbing it out, you try being good, you try going to church, maybe. But you can't get yourself clean. And the problem is, God won't let you into his heaven with a dirty soul. You have to be spotless. You show up at the pearly gates with sin on your soul and God has to turn you away. And you know what that means: an eternity separated from God and all the other good things in life. That's lonely. That's painful."

Tito pictured himself running—running away from God. Angels at the pearly gates mocking his dirty soul, and he had nowhere else to go.

"The good news," said the speaker, "is that Jesus died for our sins. The Bible says his blood cleans us up, it 'cleanses us from all sins.' By accepting Jesus as our Savior, we can have clean souls. And when we get to heaven, God will welcome us with open arms."

The speaker had them all bow their heads. He prayed a prayer and asked the kids to repeat it, if they meant it, in their own hearts. Tito had done this before, parroting Grandmother's Spanish bedtime prayers. Only this was for keeps. It wasn't "Keep me safe through the night" but "Keep me forever."

"Lord Jesus, I know I am a sinner."

Something inside of him was yelling, *How dare you call me a sinner!* But that voice faded and Tito found his conscious mind repeating the words: *Lord Jesus, I know I am a sinner.*

"And I am sorry for my sin."

Sorry? But you don't understand. If you had to go through what I have had to go through— A battle was raging in Tito's head, but the rebels were retreating. *I am sorry for my sin.*

"I accept Jesus as my Savior."

There was nothing else to say. Tito felt a wind blowing through him, pushing him across a boundary line. *I accept Jesus as my Savior.*

"Clean up all my sin with your blood."

Could that really happen? Could a bad kid like Tito stand clean before God? If so, that's what he wanted. *Clean up all my sin with your blood.*

The speaker asked those who had accepted Jesus to raise their hands. "Every head bowed. Every eye closed," the speaker directed. Tito knew very well that a dozen kids were peeking, looking around, but he didn't care. He had crossed that line in his heart. He put his hand in the air.

In the back of the room, Bill Dillon saw Tito's hand raised, and he quietly thanked God.

Tito still did bad things. He still fought. His temper would still flare up.

Only now he felt bad about it. He had a conscience. The speakers at ICI called it the Holy Spirit. Tito had a voice inside him that would whisper, *No, that's wrong. That's not who you are now. Do this instead.* Tito had cast his lot with the Christians. He had crossed the boundary line. When he did the same old misbehaving, he was on the wrong side of the fence, and he knew it. *That's not who you are now.*

He stopped stealing candy bars. But he would forge his leader's signature on the memory verse cards, giving himself credit for learning Bible verses when he really hadn't. The leaders were promising a trip to see the Barnum and Bailey Circus for kids who amassed enough points. That meant memorizing a lot of verses. Not that memorizing was hard for Tito. Verses stuck in his head after only a few readings. But why bother? Sometimes he just didn't feel like it. And if you can beat the system by forging a signature, do it just to prove you still can.

Tito wasn't taunted much anymore. His body had grown into proportion with his head, and he looked pretty normal. His athletic prowess and bold style had gained the respect of his friends. Even his enemies were careful not to set off his temper.

But insecurity gnawed at Tito from the inside. He still had to prove himself to friends and enemies alike. The force that drove him was his immense desire to be liked. Along with this was his immense fear that, if he didn't keep winning the love or respect of those around him, they would eventually realize how ugly and worthless he really was.

By the time he entered junior high, many of his buddies had joined gangs. Tito remained a free-lancer. He had always resisted authority. The authority of a gang was no different. He got involved in a few gang-related activities, but he didn't feel like going through the initiation process.

There was a new kid in Tito's seventh-grade class at Yates Junior High. He was white. There were other white kids in the neighborhood, even in the local gangs, but this kid *looked* white. He wore white-looking clothes and those brown suede "white-boy" shoes. He didn't belong at Yates. This was YLO turf. The kid looked like he belonged to the Gaylords, the predominant white gang in the area.

Tito would mock the kid mercilessly, and others would join in. Within a few weeks, Tito's friend Emilio had picked a fight with the white boy and beaten him, as Tito and other friends cheered him on. The kid went home and never returned to school.

That deed hung heavy on Tito's mind. They had succeeded in terrorizing this new kid, but what was it worth? It was all in fun, he told himself. But that whisper kept coming back: *It wasn't much fun for the white boy.*

Many of the Bible verses Tito memorized flew out of his mind shortly after he got credit for them. But some of them stuck. One was 2 Timothy 2:15, the theme verse for the Awana Clubs: "Study to show thyself approved unto God, a workman that needeth not to be ashamed, rightly dividing the word of truth."

Under all those old English words was an idea that struck deep: "approved unto God . . . need not be ashamed."

Tito knew shame; he craved approval. He thought about the times he had won approval from family or friends. Playing games and picking fights. That's how he proved himself; that's all he was good at. But when had he ever decided to do something really good? When had anything worthwhile arisen from his soul?

Shame was a hulking hound that had followed him around all his life. He had learned to live with it. The pictures flashed through his mind. His grand-mother sadly shaking her head. "*¡Un niño travieso!*"—"Such a bad boy!" The taunts of the school kids: "Ug-ly! Ug-ly!" The third grade teacher handing back the test with a big red F: "You failed again, Bonehead." And those secret shames deep within him, faces appearing in his dreams: "Don't tell anybody. This is our little secret." Wanting to cry but having no voice. "If you tell, you'll be sorry." The grime all over him, body and soul. These things weren't his fault—or were they?

Tito remembered his father looking at him after he had fallen again. His arm was already in a sling, his hand bandaged, now he had cut his head and need-ed stitches. It hurt like crazy, but he heard Dad mutter, "Are we going to have to take you to the doctor again? We can't afford this, Tito. What are we going to do with you?"

Lash out or run or bury the shame so deep inside that no one will see. That's all you can do. "Need not be ashamed"? Maybe someday.

The verses of Isaiah 53 also penetrated Tito's mind, circled and circled, and attached firmly. They fascinated him, though he found them somewhat disturbing.

> *He is despised and rejected of men; a man of sorrows, and acquainted with grief: and we hid as it were our faces from him; he was despised, and we esteemed him not.*

The leaders told him this was about Jesus. It could have been about Tito. He knew how that felt. The surrounding verses said his face was "marred," that is, spotted, perhaps pockmarked with acne. "He hath no form nor comeliness . . . there is no beauty that we should desire him." Did Jesus' childhood playmates chant, "Ug-ly! Ug-ly!"?

> *But he was wounded for our transgressions, he was bruised for our iniquities: the chastisement of our peace was upon him; and with his stripes we are healed.*

This was maddening. If he was truly the Son of God, why were they messing with him like this? He gave them no reason to be jealous. What was the problem?

> *All we like sheep have gone astray; we have turned every one to his own way; and the Lord hath laid on him the iniquity of us all.*

All the stealing, fighting, terrorizing the white boy in the brown suede shoes. This was the problem. But why deal with it like this? Why not turn us over the divine knee for a well-deserved spanking? Why not put up your dukes and teach us a lesson? Why suffer when you're God?

> *He was oppressed, and he was afflicted, yet he opened not his mouth: he is brought as a lamb to the slaughter, and as a sheep before her shearers is dumb, so he openeth not his mouth.*

He acted as if he had nothing to prove. But he was the Son of God, though nobody seemed to notice. He could have snapped his fingers and set the world on end. Why didn't he fight back?

The questions swirled in Tito's head.

9. Special Delivery

Big, strapping Paul Strzala was part of the Midwest Connection at Inner City Impact. His buddy Stanley Jay worked as a volunteer with the Humboldt Park ministry. Stan had assembled a pack of street-wise, solid Christian role models to lead the kids who came to the Awana programs. He found most of these guys, including Paul, at Midwest Bible Church at Cicero and Addison.

Paul had grown up in that church and had attended Midwestern Christian Academy, the school operated by the church. As a first grader at that school, he had become a Christian. A city kid through and through, Paul was tough, a competitor, but he'd give you the shirt off his back. He worked hard at everything he did. He even played hard, becoming quite a sportsman. And he brought that diligence to his relationships. He loved people with all he had.

Awana had provided an early outlet for Paul's competitive streak, first at Northside Gospel Center and later at Midwest. He had mastered the games: the relay, the three-legged race, the balloon toss. To the casual observer, these may seem like party games. But to Paul and his Awana cohorts, these were serious sports. Each year at the Chicago area Awana Olympics they would strive to set new records and carry home the champions' medals.

Christmas of 1978, Paul made his first appearance at Inner City Impact. Stanley Jay asked Paul to be a guest speaker for the Pioneers club, kids in sixth to eighth grades. Paul, in his early twenties, was working as a supervisor for UPS at the time. Stanley had a hunch that the boys would like this nononsense guy with his broad manner and big smile. He was right.

Paul told the Christmas story—a woman pregnant out of wedlock, a faithful husband, turned out of tenement after tenement, finally finding a stable. The kids didn't know much about mangers and hay, but they could relate to the frustration of Mary and Joseph. The little town of Bethlehem apparently wasn't all that different from the big city of Chicago. Closed doors, cantankerous authorities, fending for yourself as best you could—these city kids saw the story played out daily.

This broad-shouldered delivery man was telling the story from his gut. His high-pitched voice carried energy and excitement. The Savior of the world was born among smelly animals. Yet wise men brought their gifts. Angels sang: "Glory to God in the highest, and on earth peace to men of good will." Paul was carrying a special parcel, tidings of great joy, to a roomful of boys who would most likely grow up and become drug addicts or gang members, go to jail or die violently. "On earth, peace."

Paul looked out and measured the stares he was getting. This kid was hanging on every word, but this kid was almost asleep, and this kid was obviously thinking about something else. He wondered how many of them would ever know this promised peace.

Tito sat in the front row, joking around with his buddies.

10. Only a Game

It was a rough spring that year in Humboldt Park. War broke out between the Spanish Cobras and the Insane Unknowns. On April 13 twenty-four-year-old Ruben Perez, a member of the Unknowns, was shot and killed. In retaliation, the twenty-year-old leader of the Cobras was gunned down the next day at the gang's corner, Division and Maplewood, about five blocks from Tito's home. On April 15 the Cobras struck back, shooting Cruz Morales, aged nineteen, in front of the Unknowns' clubhouse on North Leavitt. Three days later another Unknown was found dead in his car. A few days after that a carload of Unknowns went Cobra-hunting at Hirsch and Springfield. They shot three nongang members by mistake.

Tito's older brother was involved with the Insane Unknowns. Two of his best friends had been shot.

He heard through the grapevine that he was next. To get away from the violence, he joined the U.S. Army.

Tito continued to hang out with the ICI kids. As the cold winter turned to spring, they put on their gloves and caps and headed to the ball fields. Baseball was Tito's game. He'd trot onto the diamond like a big-leaguer and mark out his turf between second base and third. He was a shortstop. With his catlike reflexes, he could snare any grounder on the left side and gun out the runner at first. His throws sometimes sailed over the first baseman's head, and he would curse himself and run to back up second. He loved the many little things of this game that can help you win: stretching a single to a double when the outfielder gets lazy on his throw-in; breaking up a double play with a hard slide; distracting a batter with well-timed infield chatter. Tito loved to win at this game.

One day, at an ICI softball game, Paul showed up again. Stanley had brought him along, hoping to get him more involved with the Pioneers. Always the sportsman, Paul would enjoy taking the field with these kids. And he might teach them a few things about how to play.

Paul was not on Tito's team. He watched from the field as Tito stroked a single, and took second on a slow grounder. On the next hit, Tito rounded third and headed for home plate. It wasn't even close; Tito would score easily. But the catcher stood in front of the plate calling for the throw. Tito bowled him over.

It was a dirty play—no need for it. Tito helped pick the kid up and said it was all in fun, but the catcher wasn't so sure. "You were in the baseline, man," Tito laughed. "I had to run you down."

The next inning, Paul hit a single. When the next batter knocked a weak grounder to the second baseman, Tito rushed over to cover second base for a force-out, perhaps a double play. He took the toss from the second baseman and prepared to fire to first. But Paul, trying to break up the double play and avenging Tito's dirty play, slid in high and hard, knocking Tito over.

Tito was on the ground, grabbing his leg and wincing. As kids gathered around, he got to his feet slowly and took a few careful steps. He could take it, he told everyone. He'd be all right.

He was faking the whole thing.

Stanley was upset. He called Paul aside and told him not to play so rough. It was only a game. It wasn't setting a very good example for these kids to go knocking them over. You just don't hit back like that. You're liable to start a fight.

But Paul didn't know any other way to play. If you don't give it your all, what's the use of doing it? Tito was asking for it. He wanted to play rough. Paul was just giving him a taste of his own medicine. There's no bad example there. Paul wasn't playing dirty, he was just playing tough. What was wrong with that?

Stanley wouldn't back down. Paul needed to learn to take it easier with these kids, not to be so competitive. But Paul couldn't play that way. He couldn't live that way. If that was the way this Awana club worked, well, maybe he'd better go somewhere else.

The kids watched as Paul picked up his glove and walked off the field. No big deal, really. Guys had gotten upset and left before. Let's play ball.

Tito had picked himself up and dusted himself off. His first reaction had been to hit back. Maybe he deserved it, but he didn't like being hit. The first rule of the streets is: Hit back. Of course, Paul was bigger than he was, and stronger. The second rule of the streets is: Choose your fights wisely; only fight those you can beat. Of course there might be other ways to beat this gentle giant. Play a joke on him. Play the innocent victim and make him feel bad for causing injury.

And then he saw Stanley talking to Paul—yelling at him, really. What he caught of the conversation was that Stanley was worried that Paul was playing too rough for Tito and the other guys, that Tito couldn't take it. That was ridiculous. Tito could take anything. Bring on all your tough-guy friends from Midwest Bible Church—I'll beat 'em. And that's what Paul was saying, pointing to Tito and saying, "He's tough. He can take it. He'll run me down next time. That's the way we play."

Suddenly Tito knew that they were playing the same game. Who else had that kind of intensity? Richard and Emilio were fun to pal around with, but they were so casual about everything. They were liable to lose interest in a game halfway through. Paul played to win; so did Tito. On the field, Paul saw Tito as an opponent and took him seriously. That's all Tito wanted.

So when Paul marched off the field, and apparently out of Tito's life, it was all wrong. Tito wanted him back. He ran after him.

"Hey, where you going?" Tito asked.

"Home," Paul muttered as he got to his car and unlocked the door.

"I'm too tough for you, huh?" Tito joked. It was a dare, the only language he knew.

Paul threw his glove in the car and looked over at the sixth-grader. "Look, I'm sorry I ran you down out there."

"No, you're not," Tito shot back.

Paul wasn't sure what to say.

Tito went on: "It's OK, man. I wouldn't be sorry either."

"Look," Paul said. "You gotta know who you're playing with. You can play hard if you want, but that kid at the plate—he didn't know what hit him."

"He was in the baseline," Tito answered.

"And you were safe by a mile," Paul retorted. "You didn't need to do it. You were showboating."

"And what were you doing?"

"I don't know," Paul said softly. "Playing God, I guess. I do that."

Now Tito didn't know what to say. "OK, Paul, next game I promise I'll leave the catcher alone," he stammered as Paul prepared to slam his car's hatchback shut. Tito suddenly grinned and put on his best

"Mr. T" voice: "Next game I'm comin' after you."

"Only if I'm in the baseline," Paul added with a bit of a smile.

"Next game, OK, man?" Tito persisted, more seriously. "You're coming back, aren't you?"

Paul thought for a moment, then let go of the hatchback and picked up his glove. "Yeah. As I recall, I'm three for three today. Let's get back before they forget about both of us." He and Tito ran back to the ball field.

11. The Olympics

ICI belonged in the A league. Paul had been watching these city kids running, jumping, frolicking through their Awana games. He had been timing them with a stopwatch. He had been taking notes. And he knew these youngsters could beat the suburban kids at any sport on the Awana docket. He knew the A league was good. Those guys from Medinah, Midwest, and Northside had grown up on Awana games. He knew the ICI kids were a bit raw, inexperienced. They would have to be trained. But they were very talented. With his coaching, they could beat anyone.

When the ICI team went to the Awana Olympics the previous year, they were in the B league. That was a mistake, as Paul saw it. At that level, the kids wouldn't take it seriously. They goofed off too much. As it turned out, they were disqualified when some boys were caught stealing some shirts. It would take some heavy persuasion to get this team in the Olympics at all, not to mention the A league.

So before he ever cracked the whip on the kids, Paul had to pull some strings with the grown-ups. He talked to Bill Dillon, he talked to Stanley Jay, and he called the administrators in suburban Rolling Meadows. He made his point. With some hesitation, the authorities let ICI into the Olympics again and put them with the powerhouses in the A league.

Paul was the Vince Lombardi of the Awana Olympics. He was the expert, the innovator, the pro. He had played the games as a boy and coached them as a teenager. He knew how to evaluate talent. And he knew how to win.

He gathered the troops together. There was Tito, fast as the wind, with catlike reflexes. His pal Richard was tall and athletic. Emilio, another tall boy, completed this central threesome. Emilio could be a troublemaker, but if his two buddies were serious about something, he'd go along. Paul identified these three Puerto Rican boys as the catalysts—they made things happen in this group.

Then there were Martin and Sergio, Mexican brothers, both quiet. Martin ran well; Sergio had striking good looks. Another "pretty boy" Mexican, Johnny Estrada, was nicknamed Erik, for his resemblance to the TV star of "Chips." Gilbert and Nelson were also brothers, quiet but diligent. They loved competing and worked hard to win. Aniba, a short, skinny Puerto Rican kid, was a bundle of energy. He'd tag along behind Tito, Richard, and Emilio.

The team reflected the racial mixture of the community: largely Puerto Rican but very inclusive. Wiley, a big black kid, showed great potential but was still a bit clumsy. Franky and Anthony Grasso were poor whites—"hillbillies," the kids called them. They were always goofing around, making people laugh. And the team had a Filipino kid, Jaime.

Discipline was essential. The only way these kids might not win, Paul figured, would be through misbehavior. Either they would dissipate their energies by goofing off or they would disqualify themselves. Paul wanted a team that would stand and sit at his command, cheer teammates to victory but be absolutely silent when necessary. He wanted a crack drill team that would show those suburbanites what "class" was.

They needed uniforms. So one Thursday night, Paul packed thirteen kids into his Datsun for a trip to the sportswear store. They were a motley mess on the way over, kids on top of kids, arms and legs hanging out the hatchback. But the next week they looked sharp in their new duds. Shirts of golden yellow, with ICI emblazoned in black. Black shorts. White socks with yellow stripes. Brand new sneakers. Paul had paid for it all.

Awana Olympic rules allowed them four practices before the semifinals, but no one said how long the practices had to be. Paul ran late into the evenings and all day on Saturdays, painstakingly training the boys in the finer points of the games.

"Gentlemen! Let's try the beanbag toss. Here, Emilio, toss this back as fast as you can. That's pretty good, but where are you standing? You have to have your feet behind the line, but you can lean forward—like this, see? Anchor yourself by putting this foot back a little, then get your hands way out front. Try it now. That's better. But why are you winding up like that? It's all in the wrists. Here, Aniba, you try it. That's it. Just flick it back and forth, with the wrists. That's all the power you need. Now let's get all fifteen of you up there. Remember, after your toss, sit down and get out of the way. We need to go right down the line. Ready? One, two, three, four, five. . . . Excellent! Try it again."

There were tricks to everything, and Paul knew them all. On the relay, you had to run around the four bowling pins. Most kids followed the circle around, but there was no need to do that at the start. Paul taught his Olympians to cut the circle on the first lap, heading straight for the first pin, thus gaining a second or two. A second shaved is a victory earned.

The three-legged race may seem like a silly party game, but Paul had it down to a science. Two guys are strapped together at the ankle, and they run around the circle twice. You need the taller guy on the outside, Paul said, and the two should run at a

slight slant. The greatest hazard is tripping over other players who have fallen, so Paul had his kids
practice jumping over other kids—even at a moment's notice.

Tito loved all this. The practices were wearying,
but Paul was a winner, and Tito appreciated that.
For once, an adult was telling Tito how good he was,
how much he could accomplish. Paul had faith in
Tito's abilities and pushed him to be even better.
Young Tito rose to the challenge.

Paul also recognized the natural leadership which
Tito possessed. He didn't even seem to realize it
sometimes, but the other kids looked to Tito for
cues. If he misbehaved, they would too. If he was
intent on winning something, they followed suit.
Paul knew that if he wanted to quiet his team down,
he only had to signal to Tito, and there would be
silence within seconds.

One night they were running the relay for the mil-
lionth time, and Tito was tired of it. Over and over,
they had practiced passing the baton, handing it
over to the next runner without missing a stride. Tito
felt he had mastered it the third time through, but
Paul insisted on trying it again. And again. And
again.

"No!" Tito finally yelled. "We've got it, Paul!
We've done it perfectly the last five times. Why do
we need to keep working on this? Let's go on to
something else. I'm not going to run this anymore."

The other boys were stunned at Tito's outburst,

but they agreed. Their weary muscles had been worked to the limit. When Tito finished his tirade, all eyes turned to Paul.

Paul himself was shocked by this apparent mutiny, and a bit hurt. Maybe he had been working the kids too hard, but they had to learn to win. And if that tired them out, tough. But this was Tito standing up against him. If it was someone else—well, other kids had temporarily bucked his authority, and it was usually Tito that got them back in line. Paul's first instinct was to yell right back at Tito, but would that solve anything? Tito would fight back and they'd have a shouting match—if not a boxing match—and the practice would be wasted.

The kids looked back at Tito. He stood his ground, gazing defiantly at Paul. Maybe he had spoken too soon. He was just tired, and his weariness had erupted into angry defiance. But now he had played his card, launched his challenge. He couldn't back down now. He had picked this fight; he would have to win it. Unfortunately, Paul might be the only person in the world who could beat him.

Paul looked around at the boys and sensed their support for their friend. No one dared to calm Tito, to offer a compromise, to say, "Just one more time, OK?" It was Tito's battle. They were just looking on.

"All right," Paul said quietly, "if that's how you feel. I thought you guys wanted to win." He was packing up his gym bag, putting the stopwatch and clipboard away. "I thought you'd want to work hard—harder than you've ever worked before—to whip yourselves into shape. You guys can break records—if you let me show you how. But apparently you don't need me. Have a good practice."

The room was silent, except for the soft pat of Paul's sneakers against the linoleum. The door thudded shut behind him.

Everyone looked at Tito. He had won, but so what? Amazingly, the mighty Paul had backed down before the great Tito. Everyone in the room came to the slow realization that Tito's victory in this showdown—so exhilarating at first—might mean that all of them, including Tito, would lose. There would be no more running of the relay tonight, maybe no more ever. No Olympics. No trophies.

It might have been one of the Grasso boys who piped up in a silly voice, "Well, coach, what do we do now?" Emilio was ambling to the corner to get his jacket. "I guess we can go home," he muttered. Tito knew Emilio well enough to read between the words. His tone of voice sent darts toward Tito. What Emilio really meant to say was, "Well, you really blew it this time, jerk."

Everything was falling apart. Tito realized that, in order to get what he really wanted, victory in these Olympics, he would have to give up. He had won, but his winning was losing. He would have to swallow his pride and go running after Paul. He would have to say he was sorry and agree to do things Paul's way. That would be hard to do, but it was the only way to truly win.

The thoughts crowded Tito's fourteen-year-old

brain as he heard the murmurs of his friends behind him. The practice was breaking up, and with it went the whole Olympic dream. This was the best thing that had happened in Tito's life to date, and he felt it disintegrating.

"No," Tito said. "Wait."

He hurried to the door. Tito figured Paul was probably just getting into his car. If he hurried, he could still catch him. Two flights down might take a few minutes for an old guy in his twenties, but Tito could fly. He flung open the door and stepped into the stairwell.

Paul was sitting there, waiting.

The Rosemont Horizon was built in the 1970s in the wide open spaces being rapidly developed northwest of Chicago. By some creative gerrymandering, Chicago managed to get this arena within its city limits, yet it was a suburbanite's dream: easy to drive to, plenty of parking, a big, bright, shiny new facility. Already the basketball powerhouse DePaul University had been playing games there.

Awana had built its headquarters in Rolling Meadows, just a twenty-minute drive on the tollway from the new stadium. So it was fitting that the Chicago area Awana Olympics would be held there. On two successive Saturdays in March they ran the semifinals and finals.

The semifinals pitted sixteen teams against each other, in groups of four. Four Awana circles marked the Horizon's floor. Each team took a color and took its place at the circle—just like they had done a hundred times before in their church gyms. But now thousands of fans cheered them on, and thousands more seats surrounded them. This was the Big Time.

Paul led the ICI team out to their appointed circle. The boys marched like Marines, single file, their golden uniforms gleaming, their sneakers in their hands. Not one of them said a word. There was only the soft pat of seventeen pairs of feet in clean white socks against the smooth, polished floor. On Paul's signal, they sat down in unison and put on their shoes.

Traction is crucial in gymnasium games. You need full power in each stride. You need to be able to turn on a dime. Every bit of dust on the floor or on your shoes could slow you down by a microsecond. So, back in the locker room, Paul had the kids carefully clean the soles of their sneakers with alcohol, removing every particle of dirt. Then they carried their shoes, so as not to pick up any dirt from the floor. When they started, there would be nothing to slow them down. It would be clean rubber on their feet against the clean waxed wood. Some of the kids ran their fingers along the shiny floor and smiled. They had nearly broken records on the gritty linoleum back at ICI—they would surely make history here.

The other teams around the circle—Medinah, Mount Prospect, Moraine Valley—stole curious glances at the boys from the inner city. These newcomers to the A league were an unknown quantity.

They looked good. They showed discipline. And they had this unnerving look in their eyes, as if they knew they were going to win.

At Paul's command, they lined up for the beanbag toss. It was all in the wrists. One by one, fourteen boys flicked the bag back to the kid in the middle and sat down. Just like they had practiced. They won.

The winners of the first event in each of the four playing circles were announced over the loudspeaker. Already limbering up for the next event, the ICI kids heard the booming voice say, "And winning the beanbag toss in Circle Number Three . . . from Chicago . . . Inner City Impact!" For many of them, it was the first time they had ever been so acclaimed. But on that day it would be the first of many victories.

Tito's next event was the three-legged race. He ran on the outside; skinny Aniba had the inside. They anticipated the starting gun perfectly. Shackled at the ankle, they made their broad strides together across the floor. Another pair fell in front of them; together they jumped right over them, without missing a stride—just like they had practiced. Twice around the circle and they won, easily.

Paul, clipboard and stopwatch in hand, came to them, beaming. "I think you have a record. The national record was 13.2. I'm pretty sure you beat it."

The announcement of the winners had some extra excitement. "The national record in the three-legged race has been broken. Congratulations to the winners in Circle Number One, with a time of 13.1 seconds. . . ." A different team was named, from one of the other circles. Tito looked at Paul in disbelief.

". . . and that record has also been broken in Circle Number Three, with a time of 13 seconds flat, by the team from Inner City Impact." Cheers rang out all around Tito. His name was in the record book.

The events went on. ICI won most all of them, setting new records in several. It wasn't even close. Amassing thirty-five points, they easily surpassed the fourteen points of the second-place team and advanced to the finals.

They were whooping and hollering on the van ride back to Chicago. "Those suburban kids didn't know what hit them! They'll be singing our praises for a long time!"

Paul motioned for quiet and adopted a mock-serious tone. "Well, I told you to go out there and win every event. You came close, but you lost a couple. So we're going to have to practice at six-thirty tomorrow morning." The boys groaned and jeered. Paul broke into a broad grin. "Seriously, guys, I'm very, very proud of all of you."

"Next week, every event!" someone yelled, and all the kids roared their approval.

The ICI gang marched into the Horizon the following Saturday ready to win. They had loaded up on carbohydrates that morning—a pancake breakfast back at the ICI building. They had practiced during the week. Some had even prayed.

This week there was one circle for the A league. The competition came down to the final four. Paul had sent scouts to watch the other circles the previous week, so he knew a bit about the other teams' strengths and weaknesses. He knew his best guys could beat their best guys in any event, but he wanted to be sure the match-ups were right.

As the Awana bigwigs offered their flowery introductions, Tito and his teammates rehearsed the events in their minds. It's all in the wrists. Anticipate the gun. Be ready to jump. Sit down when you're through.

Finally they lined up for the beanbag toss, fourteen inner-city kids standing sharp in gold and black, awaiting the sound of the starting pistol.

Bang! And the beanbag flew back and forth. Eyes focused. Bodies stretched. Wrists snapping. One by one they did their part and sat down. Of course, Tito had to grab eager Aniba by the shirt and pull him down, but otherwise it worked like a well-oiled machine. Victory: ICI.

Richard, tall and agile, was in the center for the balloon volley. But the other teams put their tall guys out there, too. The balloon was launched as in a jump ball in basketball. Richard leapt to tap it to his team. It was batted around, nearing one team's victory line, then another. The ICI kids timed their leaps, boxed out, used all the strategies Paul had given them, and eventually swatted the balloon over their line. Victory: ICI.

It was going well for ICI as they neared the intermission. They lost one event but were establishing a healthy lead. Paul wondered whether the other teams were saving their best kids for the later events, much like a long-distance runner might lag behind until the final lap. Even with a lead, he wasn't relaxing.

Time for the beanbag grab. Five beanbags—one in the center (worth two points), a one-pointer in each quadrant. Five boys from each team, each assigned a number. If "One" was called, the number one player from each squad would rush out and grab as many beanbags as possible. And so on.

Paul had worked on this again and again. The boys learned to listen for the first sound—the *w* of *one*, the *t* of *two*. Numbers four and five had to wait for the vowel sound. They were taught to rush in low to the ground, grab the center bag, then try to get two others. Run back to deposit these behind your line, then go back out, in case any other bags are left.

Martin, Richard, Tito, Nelson, and Wiley lined up for ICI on the perimeter as the bags were placed. "Five," said the starter, and Wiley lumbered into the circle. He missed the center bag, but picked up two others. Two points.

"One," said the starter, and Martin scrambled out, grabbing the center bag and one other. Three points.

"Th—," the starter started, and already Tito had

pounced. He snatched up the center bag and the one in his own quadrant. He saw a player from the red team reaching for another bag and made a dive to get there first. He did, but the other player was on top of him—and not getting up. In his hurry to get back to his line and out again for another grab, and perhaps in some instinctive anger, Tito pushed the player off of him. He pushed too hard.

"Hey! Don't play so rough!" called someone from the red team.

"Yeah, we can play like that, too!"

"You city kids want to fight? We'll show you!"

The other coach was telling his kids to cool it. Tito shrugged it off. He was playing to win. He did what he had to.

Now the coach was talking to the officials and pointing at Tito. Paul went over to join the discussion. When Paul returned, he just said, "It's all right. Just be careful out there."

The starter took an extra moment to let things settle before calling the next number. "Two," he said, and Richard sprang toward the center of the circle. He got to the bag first, but the red player gave him a body-check that knocked him down. The whole ICI team stood up in anger. Richard jumped to his feet and shoved the other player back. They squared off, ready to fight.

Paul was wildly motioning to his team to sit down, and ordering Richard to get out of the circle before he started a major brawl. That's all they needed, he thought. All that work to get them here, and now they'll be disqualified for fighting. And that would just prove to everyone that an inner-city team couldn't make it.

The team was still standing, shouting, egging Richard on. "Go on, Ricky! You can take him! Kick that white boy's butt! Show him, Ricky!"

Paul turned on them, and summoned up a vehemence they had never seen. "SIT DOWN RIGHT NOW! YOU'LL RUIN EVERYTHING!"

The boys suddenly knew he was right. They wanted to win these Olympics more than this fight. "Hey, Emilio, sit down," someone said. "Come on, guys, let's not blow it." Tito sat down and pulled Aniba down by the shirt again. Richard looked back and saw his support defusing. He backed away from his opponent and walked back to his team.

The tension cooled during intermission. Some speaker gave a talk about "running the Christian race." Something about prizes and crowns. Tito's heart was pumping fast. He was on a high. He totaled up the points in his head. No matter what the teachers said, he could do math when he wanted to. ICI had a good lead halfway through. How many more victories would they need to clinch it?

Gilbert, Aniba, and Johnny Estrada ran the sprint relay after the break. Once each around the circle. The handoffs were perfect, just like they practiced. Gilbert built a slight lead, Aniba held it, and Johnny blew the competition away. Victory: ICI.

One or two more victories would do it, Tito figured. He looked at Paul. The coach's face was still intense. It wasn't in the bag yet. If they bombed in some event, taking fourth place, they'd let the other teams right back into it.

The marathon relay involved twice around the circle for each of three runners. Emilio ran first, then Nelson. Tito was the anchor. Paul gave them a pep talk: "Don't let up now. We need to win this. You guys have been so great with this; you can set a record today." He gave them a fatherly pat on the shoulders and sent them to their positions.

Emilio got a good jump at the gun, and cut the circle as he'd been taught. But as he turned around the bowling pin, his feet slipped. He fell badly.

"Get up, Emilio!" Tito shouted. "Get back in it!" The whole team urged on their fallen mate. Surprised and a bit disoriented, Emilio climbed back to his feet and resumed the race. It took him half a lap to regain his stride, and he was already quite a bit behind.

Nelson was determined to make up the time. They hadn't lost yet. He grabbed the baton smoothly and took his first few strides with extra power.

"Come on, Nelson!" Paul called. "We can still win it. Stay with it!" Maybe he was trying too hard, but Nelson slipped at about the same place. He tried to stumble forward and regain his balance, but he too ended up on the floor.

"Get up, man!" his teammates yelled. They were discouraged, but they shouted encouragement. Quickly Nelson struggled to his feet and ran on. Even with the fall, he hadn't lost too much time.

They were in last place, but maybe Tito's blazing speed could make it up.

Tito took the baton and heard his teammates cheer him on. He tried to be careful at the spot where his friends had fallen, but he had so much time to make up. It was probably the sweat from Emilio and Nelson that made the floor so slick at that spot. Tito tripped.

Three strikes and you're out, right? Call it a loss and try to regroup for the last few events. Paul was beginning to think in these terms. But he saw a determination in Tito's face as the young runner bounced up. Tito had to win.

Tito felt an extra surge of adrenaline. His feet pounded forward. This was faster than he had ever run. He flew through his first lap, past the quadrant where his team stood cheering. They were just a gold and black blur at the corner of his vision, but he felt their pulse as they chanted, "Ti-to! Ti-to!"

He came to the slippery spot again and felt his foot fly out of control again, but he kept moving forward. Somehow his feet stayed with him. He began to pass other runners, who were tiring.

The crowd was now noticing Tito's burst of speed. They were standing and shouting as Tito headed into the last half-lap. The anchor from the red team had been leading, but now it seemed Tito was nearly even. And Tito's feet kept flying, his bright white sneakers kissing the shiny floor, flexing, and pushing forward. "Ti-to! Ti-to!" was growing louder as Tito took his last few strides toward his teammates.

He reached the finish line and threw his hands in the air in sweet victory. He had overcome the obstacles. He had won.

Paul was filled with joy, with pride, and with amazement. If Tito could only take this determination into life, what obstacles might he overcome? Tito could be a winner, a leader, a great servant of God. All he needed was a good coach. Paul put down his clipboard and threw his arms around Tito as the loudspeaker announced the victory.

It was a magic moment for Tito. He was a winner. He worked hard, strove for something, and got it. His whole body felt proud. Satisfaction was pumping through his body like blood. He tried to keep cool about it, but every few minutes he found himself grinning.

After that, the games were just academic. Three balloon events remained, and after the first one, ICI had mathematically clinched first place. They were the Awana champions. The guys shared high-fives and patted each other on the back. Paul tried to keep the team settled enough to enter the last two events. No problem. These guys still wanted to win every event they could. After the final winners were announced Paul congratulated each team member with a paternal hug. He knew they could do it. They deserved the victory.

Paul came to Emilio and Tito, put his hands on their shoulders and asked, "What were you guys doing out there on the relay? Ice skating?"

"We had it all the way," Tito joked. "We just wanted to make it exciting."

"Well, you did," Paul laughed. "You're great, guys. You did great."

That evening they all went back to the ICI building for a victory dinner. If anything could compete with the sweet taste of winning, it was the homemade lasagna baked by Paul's mom.

12. "Bonehead" Makes Good

For years afterward Tito would savor that Olympic victory. He would try to duplicate it on several occasions, but none would ever taste as sweet as those memories of triumph at the Rosemont Horizon.

Of course, Tito tumbled back into the daily grind of junior high school. He was going to Yates now, at Francisco and Cortland. It was a low tan-brick building surrounded by blacktop. A half-dozen trailers sat together on one side of the building; these were auxiliary classrooms. Humboldt Park was spawning more children than the school system had counted on.

Inside the school, it was the same old business. It didn't matter whether Tito was reading a science book or language arts—the words blurred together as his thoughts ran off to the ball field. The math teacher could be discussing the dimensions of quadrilaterals; Tito's mind would be marking the measurements of Wrigley Field. "And at shortstop today, in place of the injured Ivan DeJesus . . . Tito Matias!" The roar of the crowd dissolved back into the drone of the teacher's voice.

"So how do we determine the perimeter of a rectangle? Tito?"

"I . . . uh . . . I don't know."

"I thought so. Maria?"

He was on the perimeter all right.

One day, there was a fight. One girl was picking on another. The victim happened to be a friend of Tito's, so he stood up for his friend. He beat up the other girl.

Of course the teacher came upon the scene as Tito was administering the last few blows. Mr. Cowden, the social studies teacher, was not surprised. Tito had a reputation as a tough kid, a troublemaker. It was a shame, he thought. Each day he looked into Tito's eyes as he taught. Some of these kids just had blank stares. Some just passively received whatever he was teaching. A precious few kids had bright, eager eyes, drinking in every last fact about the American Revolution or Civil War. Tito's eyes were bright and active, but focused somewhere else. There was a drama going on inside his skull. Maybe he was fighting his own revolution.

Mr. Cowden called Tito's grandmother in for a visit. He had met with her once before, when Tito had misbehaved, but it had done little good. She spoke little English; he knew a few shreds of Spanish. He had managed to convey that Tito was a bad boy and would have to behave better—as if she didn't know already.

This time Tito would have to be there. Tito dreaded the meeting. His grandmother might hit him afterward, as she had done before. But it was more than that he feared. He hated the perplexed stare she would give him, the shake of the head. "What am I going to do with you?" He hated to disappoint her, but it seemed he always did.

They met after school one day in the classroom. Grandmother wedged herself into one of the desks, and Tito sat in the next one. Mr. Cowden perched on the edge of his desk.

"Tito," he said, "you're going to have to tell your grandmother exactly what I'm telling you. I need you to translate, but it won't do any of us any good if you change it. Do you understand?"

Tito nodded solemnly.

Mr. Cowden looked straight at Grandmother. She peered back through her wire-rim glasses.

"Tito was fighting again," he began. Before Tito could translate, she was nodding. She knew those words. She had heard them before.

"I don't know what to do about him," he continued. She nodded again.

"He is not doing well in my class or in any class." These words, too, were familiar. She looked down and appeared to study the carvings on the desk surface.

"It doesn't have to be this way," Mr. Cowden went on. Tito dutifully translated and his grandmother looked up. "I believe Tito is a very bright boy. If he worked hard, if he studied, he could get an *A* in my class."

Tito stopped, mid-sentence. He had never heard this before. Mr. Cowden looked earnestly at him. "Yes, Tito, I mean it. If you applied yourself, you could do it. I'm sure of it. Tell her. Go on, tell her."

The boy slowly recast the words in Spanish for his grandmother. She gave the teacher a curious look. Was Tito translating right, or was he just making himself look good?

"*A*?" she asked, pronouncing the vowel halfway between Spanish and English. Mr. Cowden stood up and went to the chalkboard. In three strokes he drew it. "A"—big as life.

"Do you really think so?" Tito asked. Ever since his third grade teacher called him "Bonehead," he had assumed he was. Whenever he picked up a schoolbook, a voice inside him said, "Put it down, Bonehead. You're bound to fail at this. Why try?" And here was a teacher telling him the opposite.

"You're a smart kid, Tito. You'll have to work to get that *A*, but you can do it. I'm here to help you."

Tito felt a smile creep to the corners of his lips. This hadn't turned out as either he or his grandmother expected. Her voice surprised him. "And the fighting?" she asked in hesitant English.

"I don't think fighting is the real problem here," the teacher told them both. "What Tito did was bad.

He deserves to be punished for it. But maybe if he succeeds in class, he won't have to fight so much. Do you hear me, Tito?"

The boy nodded.

"I'll tell you what. We have a Constitution test coming up in a week. I want you to study for that like you've never studied before. If you do well on that test, let's forget about the fighting. All right?"

Tito translated for his grandmother. She looked askance at the teacher. His warm face was pleading, in a way, "Let's take a chance on this kid." She turned toward Tito, the boy she loved but couldn't control, and back to Mr. Cowden. "Thank you," she said softly.

"We the people of the United States, in order to form a more perfect union, establish justice, insure domestic—what is that next word?"

"Tranquility," Luis answered. "What on earth does it mean?"

"Peace," Tito said. "I looked it up."

"How much longer do you have to do this? Let's play ball."

"Just a little more, man."

A week later Tito brought home his Constitution test. On the top Mr. Cowden had scrawled his score—98—and a red *A*. Big as life.

13. A Secret Storm

That summer Tito went to camp. He was fourteen, about to enter his freshman year at Roberto Clemente High School.

He had had a good year, learning a lot about himself. The Olympic victory still gave him a rush of satisfaction as he remembered it. And Mr. Cowden had shown him that he had a good mind, too. But the teacher had been wrong about one thing: the fighting didn't stop. Tito was still quick to take a dare, to lash out against an opponent, to get even. It was as if he expected people to mistreat him, and he'd be ready when they did. His temper would ignite with the slightest spark. And he still felt an enormous pressure to prove himself. There was a storm raging in his soul, and it created an intensity in everything he did.

It was good to get out of the city for a while, especially in the summer. Humboldt Park gets hot—and violent. Kids out of school cluster in parks and on street corners. Gangs recruit. Drug dealers step up their business. Street warriors strut their stuff, wave their weapons. You never know when a car might pull up beside you with a gun aimed at your chest—merely for wearing the wrong colors or walking on the wrong block.

Phantom Ranch camp, an hour and three-quarters' drive north, in Wisconsin, offered a temporary oasis. There was lots of room there—room to run, to play, to grow, to dispel whatever phantoms might be haunting you.

Paul knew practically everyone at Phantom Ranch. He had worked there for many summers. At his urging, and through his string-pulling, Tito attended camp as a "counselor in training."

The counselors must have wondered what they were training Tito to become. He seemed to resist at every step. Sure, he had leadership potential. As long as he could do what he wanted, he would do it with assurance and savvy, inspiring others. But Tito still had an authority problem. Ask him to do things your way, and he'd buck you.

Mark Hankins was the counselor for Tito's cabin. Built like a fireplug—only five-foot-six, he played football for North Park College—he wouldn't stand for any nonsense. But underneath the tough demeanor was a caring heart. He cared enough to demand the best from these guys, and they respected him for it.

Except for Tito. With Tito it was always a fight. "Come here"—he'd go there. "Sit down"—he'd stand up. "Stand up"—he'd walk away. Tito was shrewd enough to use the system to beat the system. He knew just how much he could get away with—and even then he'd cross the line just to prove he could. Tito was just a bad kid.

Curfew was nine-thirty. Lights out. In bed. Quiet. But Tito was making noise, telling jokes, horsing around with the other kids. Of course, that got the whole cabin going.

The lights went on. Mark Hankins was standing there, with that drill-sergeant look on his face. "Put on your clothes, gentlemen. You're going running." The boys, caught in midact, groaned. They pulled on their jeans and T-shirts and headed outside.

"The hill?" asked one young camper.

"The hill," Mark said, to another collective groan.

Phantom Ranch had a hill. It was no Everest, but it could sure tire you out to run up and down it ten or fifteen times. The kids from the cabin knew this well. With Tito stirring them up, they seemed to have more than their share of jogs on the hill. Going down could actually be fun—feeling the wind in your face, letting gravity and momentum pull you, flying late at night out of control. Chicago doesn't have hills.

But going up was a drag. Lifting one knee after the other until they could hardly move, feeling the muscles strain in the backs of your thighs and

CHILD OF THE CITY

calves, nearly doubled over. Up and down, up and down, until Mark decided you'd had enough.

Tito liked to run. His legs were strong. He seemed to have the energy of five kids. While the others were dragging their bodies up the hill for the fifth or sixth time, Tito held his head high. He loved this hill. With each confident stride he was saying, *Thank you, Mark, for letting me run this hill. This was my plan all along.* While the other boys were atoning for their sins, Tito was writing his own law, the Law of Tito: *Everyone will mistreat you. Don't let them win.*

After forty-five minutes or so, Mark called them in. The boys plodded into the cabin, peeled off their clothes, and crawled into bed. They were far too tired to misbehave, but for good measure, Mark added a final warning: "Now if I hear one more word, you've had it."

Tito couldn't let him win. Maybe everyone else was weakened into submission, but not Tito. The moment Mark flicked off the lights, Tito piped up in a mocking nasal voice, "Now if I hear one more word . . . ." The cabin was filled with stifled giggles.

The lights went on. "Tito!" Mark roared. "Get out here! Now!" Defiantly, the boy swung down from his bunk and began putting on his jeans. "Now!" Mark ordered. "Just as you are!"

Tito put down the jeans and strode outside in his underwear. "I take it you haven't had enough exercise," Mark began, as they walked toward an open area away from the cabin. "I don't understand you, Tito. Why do you do this?"

The boy didn't say a word, but just walked with the counselor. Then they stopped, and Mark told Tito to do some jumping jacks. "Sure," he replied nonchalantly. He began jumping, flapping his arms over his head. These were sharp, regimented moves, armylike. Tito enjoyed doing jumping jacks. He would do them well.

After about fifty of them, Tito saw that Mark wasn't paying much attention, but looking off into the distance. "Do you want me to stop?"

Mark turned briefly. "No, keep going," he said, and turned away again, looking up into the broad Wisconsin sky. Perhaps he was praying.

When Tito had done about fifty more jumping jacks, Mark asked, "Are you tired yet?"

It was a dare. *Don't let him win.* Tito laughed, "I can do this all night."

"All right."

Tito continued his crisp motions, feet out, feet together, hands up, hands down. He was beginning to tire, but he'd never admit it.

Mark began to talk. "What makes you so tough, Tito? Why are you fighting all the time? You always fight, Tito. You fight me, you fight the other kids, you fight Paul. Why do you do it?"

Tough guys don't answer dumb questions. Tito kept jumping. He got sort of a second wind and renewed his efforts. *Ha!* he thought. *Mark will wear out before I do.*

And Mark did seem to be bothered as he looked down at the ground, shaking his head. He would look up at Tito's bobbing head and look down again. He wasn't angry, just troubled.

"You never listen to us, Tito. Why is that? We tell you to do something and you do the opposite. Why? We tell you to stop doing something bad and you keep doing it, even if you don't really want to do it. Why, Tito? What makes you so bad?"

Tito was tiring. He kept jerking his mind back to the present moment, this night, this camp, these movements. But he kept thinking about Chicago. Scenes from first grade, second grade, entered his mind. "Ug-ly! Ug-ly!" The kids would taunt him. And he would run away.

His bare feet were pounding the dirt of Phantom Ranch, but inside he felt his sneakers pounding pavement, running away from the taunts. *Nothing, nothing, nothing*—each step beat the message through his body. *You're nothing, nothing. You don't matter, you don't count. You're ugly, ugly, ugly.*

And Mark was asking, "Why, Tito? Why?" And Tito's heart raced. He saw the faces of teachers— "Sit down and be quiet!" *You're nothing, Tito. You have nothing to say.* He saw his classmates—"Ugly! Ugly!" He wanted their love, but he wasn't worthy of it. He could only inspire fear. He saw his family, and friends of the family—those so-called friends. "Don't tell anybody. This is our little secret." And the awful pain inside him, and the guilt. Who would he tell? The guilt ate him alive. But who could he tell? He was nothing, nothing. No one would believe him, no one would care.

Tito felt his cheeks wet with tears. The breeze blew gently against his face, drying them. He kept jumping, and the pictures kept filling his head. Pictures of himself, looking in the mirror, peering at his pockmarked skin, his yellowed teeth. *Ugly, ugly. I'm nothing*.

And the greasy mechanic that awful day. "Come here, boy." He was numb. He was a corpse. All feeling was siphoned out of him. He wanted to run.

His mind ran back to the present, to camp, to his body, growing numb with the effort, and Mark still pressing him. "Why, Tito?" Tears were streaming down Mark's cheeks, too. Something was happening here, there was nowhere to run. "Why are you so bad, Tito?"

"YOU DON'T KNOW HOW IT FEELS!" Tito blurted out.

"What?" Mark asked. "How what feels?"

"To be nothing! To be ugly!"

"What do you mean?" Mark was still pushing. He wouldn't let him go.

Tito stopped his jumping. He made no effort to wipe the tears from his face. "I was raped, twice, by—by so-called friends of the family."

"Tell me about it."

It had happened when Tito was eight. The first "friend" was nineteen or so. He used to come over and watch TV at Tito's house. One night there was no one else home. Just Tito.

It began as a game. A secret game. "Don't tell

anybody," the guy said. Tito liked games, but the game got strange, perverse. And soon the guy was forcing himself on young Tito, using him sexually.

Afterward Tito felt numb. He was afraid that he had done something very wrong. He was always doing wrong things, and this perversity—it must have been his fault. He couldn't tell his parents. What could they do? They would probably blame Tito, the kid who was always doing bad things. Of course he couldn't go to the police. They never helped anyone—not in Humboldt Park.

It was a secret game, all right. The secret festered inside of Tito. He played games of guilt within himself.

About four months later it happened all over again. Tito helped out at a garage next to his house. One evening the mechanic was working late and Tito was with him. The man was much older, in his forties or beyond. The light outside the garage windows was fading to dusk. The bare bulb hanging from the open hood of the car sidelit the man's face as he turned his lustful gaze toward young Tito. "Come here, boy." Tito sensed it in his voice. It would be awful, but what could he do? "If you tell, you'll be sorry." He was sorry already. He felt the man's grimy hands on him, the grime seeping into his skin, becoming part of him.

Tito didn't remember the details, just that he felt like garbage. Worse than garbage—nothing. He didn't feel anything at all. It was almost expected now. The nineteen-year-old, the mechanic, and everyone else in the world could use and abuse him. He would just have to take it.

For months afterward Tito did not wash his face. He was dirt; why wash? The grease of that garage was inside him—washing did no good. He was still worth nothing. He would look in his mirror and hate himself. *They're right. I'm ugly.*

14. The Road Back

For five years Tito had held his secret shame inside. It simmered within him. He was a pressure cooker, blowing off steam at the slightest provocation. Every insult was a threat to his manhood. His very personhood was always at issue. The fighting, the stealing, the back talk had all been desperate attempts to say, "I matter!"

It would be nice to be able to say that Tito's problems were solved when he raised his hand at that ICI meeting and became a Christian. Christ does change people's lives, and he changed Tito's—but not overnight. Tito entered God's kingdom as a troubled, self-hating brawler. It would take some work to mold him into Christ's image.

The Olympic victory was a valuable start. So was the encouragement of dear Mr. Cowden. These experiences helped Tito to see that he did matter, that he could succeed. The rapes had forced him into a sort of nothingness. He was beginning to wriggle out of that.

But he still didn't trust people. Those lonely days and weeks after the first rape had branded him with a motto: *Look out for yourself. No one else will.* Authority figures were no help at all. All they wanted was power over you. Keep the power. Rule your own life. Trust only yourself.

And still Tito had nursed his dark secret. If people knew about his being raped, they would realize how dirty he really was. He could pretend to be somebody, he could be the star athlete or the good student. But it was all a show. He couldn't trust people with his real self. He couldn't open up.

So Tito had lived his life for those five years, closed tight like a fist. Not giving, not receiving, only brandishing his own power.

There, under the wide Wisconsin sky, Tito had reached a breaking point. Weary from all the exercise, he unclenched his soul. He tearfully told his story to a caring counselor. And Mark Hankins honored his trust.

Tito was less resistant after that. For the rest of camp, he was quieter, more docile. The old habits were still there. He'd fly off the handle occasionally. But he was generally more relaxed, more open.

It had taken five years for him to learn to hate

himself so thoroughly. Recovery would take a while. He had accumulated many layers of bad attitudes and habits that would have to be excavated. But things would get better.

15. Buck Rogers Goes to High School

Roberto Clemente was an all-star baseball player for the Pittsburgh Pirates. He was also Puerto Rican. In the 1960s he was one of few Puerto Ricans in the national limelight. His brilliant career and his inspiring life were cut short in a tragic plane crash in 1972.

In the fall of 1980, Tito Matias found himself at Roberto Clemente High School. It was a glorious structure: a nine-story block of modern architecture, broad windows framed by sharp black girders. The city had put out $30 million to build the thing in 1974. At the time it was the second most costly high school building in the state. It looked something like a prison.

The structure was designed to hold thirty-one hundred students. By the time Tito got there, there were well over four thousand.

Gangs ran rampant in the school. In the hallways, lavatories, and classrooms, they recruited members, terrorized opponents, sold drugs. The Latin Disciples, Latin Kings, Spanish Cobras, Dragons, and others vied for power. The incoming freshman got a quick education in the signals and colors and territorial rights of each of these gangs. There were certain areas of the school you learned to avoid. When the bell rang, you either got into a classroom or prepared for a fight. It was a matter of survival.

The first day of school, there was a major fight: a girl was viciously beaten up by two other girls. Each day security guards patrolled the school entrance and checked students' IDs. If they thought you were carrying a gun, they'd frisk you roughly.

Tito, as always, was his own man. The gang presence at school created some fear in him, but it also gave him a challenge. He could play this game and win, he decided. He hung around with the Dragons but didn't join. He went out for the football team, made some enemies, and quit. He'd pick fights with anyone, gang member or not. He used to imagine himself as Buck Rogers: getting himself into jams but winning the day with wit and finesse.

Good grades came easily that year; there wasn't much to it. The classes were easy—boring, in fact. No one else tried very hard. The dropout rate for the school at the time was over 70 percent. Tito skipped classes regularly. If they caught him playing hookey, so what? What could they do, send him home? With minimal study, Tito made the honors club. He went to one meeting and was bored out of his mind.

Paul was spending more and more time with him, calling him after school, coming over on Saturdays. Tito appreciated the attention; he was losing touch with his old pals Emilio and Richard. Oh, he saw them in the halls at school, but they had different classes, different schedules. They were making different friends. Though he'd never admit it, Tito was lonely. He needed Paul's easygoing friendship.

Grandmother moved back to Puerto Rico at the beginning of Tito's freshman year. A relative had taken sick, so she went to care for him. That left Mom and Dad to care for Tito. But generally he fended for himself.

It was not a good time in the Matias household. Mom and Dad were having difficulties with each other, leaving little time or energy for their troublesome sons. They were glad that their eldest, Ricky, had made it through adolescence, despite his gang involvement, and into the army. Luis, still in junior high, was already beginning to run with the gangs. Tito, however, was a mystery. One day he'd be memorizing Bible verses; the next he'd be pounding some guy's face in. What would ever become of him?

Spring of 1981 brought a rush of new activity, positive and negative. As a ninth-grader, Tito couldn't compete in the Awana Olympics for the ICI team. Yet he longed to relive that championship experience. He learned that Northside Gospel Center had an Awana program for older kids, so he grabbed his old teammate Nelson, and the two of them took a half-hour bus ride each Monday evening. They played the games, memorized the verses, and made the Northside Olympic team.

Tito also talked Luis into joining the ICI team. On Thursday nights, he would help the new coach with that team. He was the expert now, taking what Paul had taught him and passing it on to another "generation." He liked that.

The Olympics went well on both counts, but the experience couldn't match the first time. The ICI team once again swept the A league, with Luis and Wiley leading the way. In the high-school-age Olympics that followed, the Northside team struggled through the semifinals, then made it to the finals and won the trophy. Tito was trying too hard. In the semifinal relay, he knocked over a pin—causing a costly penalty—and threw a temper tantrum, beating the floor with his fists. When his team finally won, however, Tito hammed it up for the audience, kissing the trophy and waving.

Luis picked a fight that spring with a member of the Latin Disciples. Tito saw the whole thing, and eventually pulled his brother off the other guy. But the Disciple was shouting curses and threats at both of them. "I'll get my friends after you! I'll get the whole gang! You'll be sorry!" Unfortunately, this guy and his friends went to Clemente with Tito—Luis was still in junior high—so Tito bore the brunt of these threats. He was regularly berated, baited, and threatened. Tito learned to watch his step, to come straight home after baseball practice, to avoid the Disciples' turf at school and in the neighborhood.

Paul rescued Tito from a lot of that. They'd go to a movie or out for ice cream or to a Cubs game, and for a while Tito was free from all those worries. Paul would ask whether Tito was praying and reading his Bible. Tito tried to do this regularly—sometimes it was hard. Paul asked if Tito was getting any better at controlling his temper. Sometimes Tito lied and said yes. But Paul was there to listen to Tito's gripes about his father, about school, about the gangs. And he was there to share Tito's fun.

Coming out of the movie *E.T.*, Paul was a mess, tears rolling down his cheeks. Tito was amused that this rough, tough, street-smart guy would be so touched by a dumb movie. He teased him. "I bet you cry at *Star Wars*, too. Boo-hoo! The Empire's striking back!"

They went to Baskin-Robbins for some ice cream afterward. "So, Tito," Paul asked as he stole the cherry from his sundae, "what's new in the neighborhood?"

Tito got serious all of a sudden. "Well, I don't know if you heard this, but did you know Emilio was arrested?"

"No. When?"

"Last week. Weapons possession."

"What's going to happen?"

"I don't know," Tito answered. "He's been in trouble before. They might send him to juvie."

Paul shook his head. He knew the juvenile detention center would only make things worse for Emilio. He'd learn to be a better criminal. "I wondered why we hadn't seen him around lately."

"I haven't seen him much myself. He's been hanging with the gang a lot. Getting into a lot of stuff."

"I wish we could have done more with him," Paul mused. "I was never sure if we were getting through. I still remember you, Emilio, and Richard sitting in the front row cracking jokes while I was trying to talk."

"Would I do that to you?" Tito asked in mock innocence.

"Every chance you got," Paul shot back. "The problem was, some of your jokes were pretty funny, and I wanted to laugh, but I couldn't because I was up there speaking." He thought for a moment. "Although I'm really not sure if my speaking did any good."

"Yeah, it did," Tito said very seriously. "Some of it got through."

Both dug into their ice cream for a few spoonfuls. Then Paul looked up. "Do you ever see Richard?"

"Not much. I heard he was sick."

"Real sick?"

"Yeah," Tito muttered. "That's what I hear. He hasn't been at school for a couple weeks."

"What is it?" Paul wondered. "Mono?"

"I heard it was hepatitis."

"Oh no."

Tito nodded his head slowly. "Dirty needles, I guess."

Paul looked at his friend in silence for a few minutes.

"The three of us," Tito finally said, determined not to cry. "We used to be a team. The three Moosketeers. All for one and one for all. Now Richard's sick from his drugs. Emilio's in jail. What's going to happen to me?"

Tito looked up with big eyes. The veneer was gone. Paul could see he was scared to death.

"Don't worry, Tito. You'll be all right. God and I will make sure of that."

16. Blessed Are Those Who Mourn

Richard looked yellow. His once strong body was skin and bones. It pained Tito to look at him.

The hospital surrounded them with its white sterility. It smelled of antiseptic. Richard lay back in bed in his single room and smiled weakly at his friend. Tubes ran from hanging bags into his arms, which rested motionless at his sides.

Stanley Jay was there, too, standing at the foot of the bed and looking on as Tito talked with his old pal. Paul was out of town.

"Thank you for coming," Richard said. His voice was low and whispery, not the boisterous Richard of old. Tito sat on the edge of the bed and looked into his friend's eyes. They were yellow, too.

"Sorry I didn't come sooner. I bet all the other guys have been here already."

"No," Richard said. "You're the only one. Just

Paul and Stanley." His eyes drifted up gratefully to where Stanley stood.

"Oh," Tito mumbled. What do you say in a situation like this? "So, Richard, how are you doing?" He said it, and knew it was all wrong.

Richard smiled weakly and moved his head in the general direction of the bags and tubes that were feeding him. "Not too bad . . . considering."

"Yeah," Tito answered. "Well, it looks like they're taking pretty good care of you."

"Yeah." Another awkward pause.

"Did you hear about the Olympics this year, man? They won again."

"Yeah," Richard said softly. "Paul told me."

"You should have seen it. Luis was on the team this year. He's almost as fast as me."

Richard smiled again. "Almost," he repeated.

"Maybe next year, Richard. You and me can help Paul coach the team, huh? You'll be up and out of here in no time. We'll have fun."

"Tito," Richard said carefully. "I'm going to die."

Tito grabbed his friend's hand. He had never touched him like that before. Forget machismo, Tito needed to hold Richard's hand. "No, Richard," he said with an empty laugh. "No. You can't die. You'll be all right. I know it."

A nurse came in and announced it was time to go. Richard squeezed Tito's hand with all the strength he had. "Thank you," he said faintly.

Tito left the room, shaken, but confident that Richard would recover.

A few weeks later Tito had a run-in with some Latin Disciples. They chased him, threatening. He needed to get away. Could he escape to camp again this summer? He called Stanley, who arranged for Tito to work in maintenance at Phantom Ranch. Days later, he was safe in Wisconsin.

At camp Tito received word that Richard was in a coma. At first the news jolted him. He was so sure Richard would get better. Now it was almost certain he would die. Tito wished Paul was around—he would say the perfect thing. But Paul was busy back in Chicago, driving a bus all night for the transit authority. So Tito had to face this alone. How would Buck Rogers handle it? He'd take it in stride. He'd keep a stiff upper lip. He would go on about his business, do what had to be done.

Working in the kitchen that day, Tito began to cry. Tears flooded his eyes, rushed down his cheeks, dripped into the dishwater. Richard would soon be gone, and he would take with him a chunk of Tito's past. They had built a world together—Richard, Emilio, and Tito—a world of games and fantasies. They had helped each other grow up. They had shared the secrets of survival in their crazy community. But those secrets of survival weren't helping.

Richard had learned to be cool. His athletic ability brought him respect. But coolness apparently included drugs. And the hepatitis virus apparently didn't care what kind of athlete he was. Emilio had learned to be tough. His don't-mess-with-me attitude got him through a lot of scrapes. But it also landed him in jail. At least he was alive—but for how long?

As Richard lay in a Chicago hospital, slowly giving up the fight, Tito was closing the door on his old life. In his mind he summoned up the memories of the good times those three buddies had shared. And he said good-bye. Things would never be the same again.

It was as if the tears were flushing out his past. Helpless, he let them go. The memories rushed down his face and into the sudsy sink.

The head cook, Ma Johnson, noticed Tito's tears and asked if she could help. She was a grandmotherly type, a caring Christian lady. She took Tito in her arms and cradled him there, sympathizing with his pain, reassuring him that God would work things out. They prayed together, there in the kitchen, for miraculous healing, if that was God's will; for comfort for Richard's family and friends; for strength for Tito to deal with this crisis.

A week or two later, the camp manager invited Tito over to his house. This seemed a bit strange to Tito, since he had always thought that Roy didn't like him. Tito was always bending or breaking rules, and Roy, in his role as camp manager, was always scolding him. On this morning, however, Roy was quiet, even somber, as he sat across from Tito in his living room.

"Tito, there comes a time in everyone's life when they have to face up to certain—"

"Are you trying to tell me Richard's dead?" Tito interrupted.

Roy nodded. He crossed to where Tito was sitting and put his arm around him. He wasn't sure what else to say.

"If there's anything I can do for you, Tito, just let me know. And you don't need to work today if you don't want to. We'll cover for you."

"Thanks," Tito mumbled. "I'll be all right." He ran back to his cabin.

The place was empty. Ten bunk beds, most of them neatly made, assorted bags and suitcases, books, half-written letters home. The other workers were out doing their jobs. Tito felt very alone in this vacant cabin. He flung himself onto an upper bunk and lay facedown. The tears came again.

The miraculous healing hadn't happened. Death was a cold reality. Tito had laughed at it back in the hospital room. He had felt its icy grip on Richard's hand, but still he insisted it wouldn't happen. Richard would beat it, as he had beaten so many foes before. They were winners, the three of them.

If only he had stayed with Richard. . . . But what good would that have done? Richard had been almost too weak to talk anyway. Tito had done his best, he had been there when the other friends hadn't. He had even touched Richard's hand. But he couldn't pull him back.

Why? Why would God let this happen? If God was really in charge of things, he was awfully cruel. To take someone like Richard in the prime of life—

before the prime of life. How dare God fight dirty like that!

And Tito thought of the others who had died in Humboldt Park, people he had heard of. A gang shooting here, a drug overdose there. Friends of friends had gone down, but never anyone so close. Yet these were all young people. God let all of this happen. How could he?

"*God is love.*" The memory verse floated into Tito's head. "*Nothing can separate us from the love of God.*" It didn't seem real, now. *How could a loving God kill Richard?* "For God so loved the world . . ." Tito remembered the speaker telling each kid to put his own name there. "For God so loved Tito . . ." And Richard was sitting right beside him that day. He heard him repeat, "For God so loved Richard . . ." But now it seemed like a bad joke.

Did Richard ever believe it? Tito had raised his hand and asked Jesus into his heart. Richard had teased him about it. They never talked much about God. Richard went to the same meetings as Tito, heard the same speakers. Paul, especially, had told them both about Jesus and what a personal relationship with Jesus could do. It could change your life, Paul had said. And Richard said his life was fine. Why should he change it? Paul had talked about heaven and hell. Heaven had always seemed sort of boring, but Paul made it sound wonderful: Cubs games and hot fudge sundaes and being with people you really, really liked. Where was Richard now?

Getting his trophies at the Awana Olympics in the sky? Tito was afraid that Richard had never become a Christian in his heart. He tried not to think about it.

"Tito, there you are."

He heard a familiar voice.

"Come on outside."

Tito looked up from his soggy pillow. It was Paul, standing in the center of the cabin.

"What are you doing here?" he asked. It was like a dream.

"Let's talk," Paul said, turning to walk outside. Tito bounded down to join him.

They walked together across the camp grounds to the baseball field. The two of them sat down on the pitcher's mound.

"As I was driving here this morning," Paul began, "a Bible verse kept coming into my head. It's Romans 8:28. Did you ever learn that one?"

"I don't know."

"It says, 'And we know that all things work together for good to them that love God, to them who are the called according to his purpose.' You have to learn this verse, Tito. It's great."

"I think I did, a couple of years ago."

"Well, learn it again. And repeat it to yourself when things . . . well, when things go crazy, when you're really hurting." Paul looked over at his friend. Tito's head was down, his fingers were scraping the soft dirt.

"You're probably pretty messed up over Richard," Paul continued. "You're probably asking a lot of questions: 'Why did God do this?'"

Tito looked up suddenly. "How did you know?"

"I know." Paul smiled. "I've been there. I mean, I've never lost a close friend like that, but lots of times things happen that you don't want. Your world is caving in and you wonder what God is doing."

"Yeah," Tito responded, taking a handful of dirt and sifting it between his hands.

"But Romans 8:28 says that God knows what he's doing, and it's going to be all right. It works together for good, for your good, even though you may not understand how. God loves you, Tito. And he has a purpose for you. We may not know what that is, but we know things are going to work out."

Tito threw down his handful of dirt and looked Paul square in the eye. "Did God love Richard?"

"Yes, of course."

"Then how could he let him get so messed up?"

Paul shook his head slowly. "Oh, Tito. I don't know. Ask him yourself. God does so much to get us out of the jams we get into. Sometimes, I guess, he's had enough." Paul stopped to choose his words carefully. "Richard had his chances to turn around. God gave him a lot of opportunities."

"Do you think he ever became a Christian?"

"I think maybe he did."

Tito's eyes darted up to Paul's. "Really?"

"I don't know what was going on in his heart. I went to see him in the hospital and told him once again about Jesus. It was the same thing he had heard at ICI for years, but he was really listening this time. I think he knew he was about to die. The Bible says that God's Word will not return void, that it will accomplish its purpose, and I can't help but think that God's Word may have finally sunk into Richard's heart."

"I hope so."

Paul took Tito's hand, briefly, just as Tito had held Richard's. "I know, Tito," he said quietly. "I know."

Tito looked up at his friend's face. It was wet with tears.

Surely he hath borne our griefs, and carried our sorrows. Snatches of Bible verses raced through Tito's mind. *A man of sorrows, and acquainted with grief.* Paul was shouldering Tito's sorrow, just as Jesus had borne his sin. *Blessed are those that mourn, for they shall be comforted.* God himself mourned for his wandering loved ones, and offered comfort to hurting people—who could then comfort others. *I am the resurrection and the life.* In Jesus, life could go on. It would go on. All things would work together for good according to his purpose, whatever that was.

The summer sun stood high in the sky and poured its warmth on the young man and boy who sat on the mound in the diamond. Paul cracked a joke; Tito smiled. Paul teased; Tito laughed. Just a few moments earlier he had wallowed in grief and self-pity, but now Tito was enjoying his friend's company.

Paul checked his watch. "I'm afraid I have to get back home," he said. "Gotta work tonight."

Tito stared in amazement. "Do you mean to tell me you drove a bus all night, got up early, drove two hours here just to see me, and now you're going back to work?"

"It's nothing." Paul shrugged. "I thought you might need some support."

17. Getting Out

Paul surveyed the situation. Just a year earlier, he had seventeen kids. He was their coach, but also, in a way, their dad. He bought them uniforms. He taught them. He disciplined them. He took them out to eat.

He had quickly learned that it's tiring—and expensive—to be a surrogate parent to so many. He very intentionally narrowed his scope to three, the three who had the most potential, and the most needs. Jesus had his Peter, James, and John. Paul Strzala had his Emilio, Richard, and Tito.

These were the guys who used to sit in the front row and tell jokes when Paul was speaking. These were the guys who were always cheating, stealing, or fighting. These were the guys who broke into Paul's car, taking his tape deck. Paul had been pretty steamed at first; he was tempted to quit. But as he thought about it, he realized that these three kids were more important than his listening pleasure. He didn't say a word about it; he just worked them harder at the next Olympic practice. And these guys turned out to be the ones who led the Olympic team to victory. They had a spark in them. If it were fanned just right, these guys could be on fire for the Lord.

This was no episode of "My Three Sons." The city is tough on kids. Paul wished he could be there, round the clock, to help these three say no to drugs and guns and gangs. But no, they had to make their own decisions. Paul faced the frustration that any parent feels. He watched as Richard, then Emilio, drifted away from his influence.

"Go to camp," he had told them the previous summer. It would get them out of that wicked city, boiling over with vices. They might avoid the gang recruiters, the pushers, the random bullets for at least one more year. They might learn to pray, to depend on God, to catch a vision of who they could become. "Go to camp," Paul said. "I'll get you in, I'll pay your way."

"No," said Emilio, after hemming and hawing for weeks. "No," said Richard. There was too much to do in the city. Too much action. Wouldn't want to miss it.

If they only knew what they had missed. Only Tito went to camp, and it had changed his life. Doing jumping jacks under the broad sky, he had chased a skeleton out of his closet. He had had a resurrection of sorts.

During their freshman year at Clemente High, Richard and Emilio slid farther away. Paul tried to hang on, but his phone calls went unanswered. They were "too busy" to get together. They weren't interested in talking about God.

And then there was one: Tito. Paul knew that Tito was on the edge. He was trying hard to be a good Christian, but the pressures of school, of the neighborhood, of old habits, weighed heavy. It was a tug-of-war: an army of pushers and gang members had Tito by one arm, pulling him down. But Paul and a host of angels were pulling the other way, slowly inching Tito into the kingdom. Paul wondered where Tito would be if he hadn't gone to camp the previous year, if, like his friends, he had craved the city's action. He might have drifted away, too. But God had other plans.

Now Tito was at camp again. Richard had just died, and Tito seemed ready to bury much of his own past. Paul came away from Phantom Ranch after visiting Tito with a sense of impending newness. Tito was ready for a new adventure. It was like cracking open a book and staring at the title page. A whole new world awaited. What would it be like?

Paul was developing a plan. He had to get Tito out of the city. He couldn't let Humboldt Park wreak its ravages on Tito as it had on his buddies. Tito wasn't strong enough for that—not yet.

Clemente was a joke. Tito wouldn't get a good education there. Paul remembered the financial sacrifice of his own parents in sending him to a private Christian school. He was willing to do the same for Tito. But where? There was Midwestern Bible Academy, Paul's alma mater. But that was too close. Tito would still live at home, subject to the temptations of the neighborhood. Maybe he could go out to the suburbs, out to Wheaton Christian, twenty-five miles west. No, Tito would go crazy in squeaky clean suburbia. He'd be back in Humboldt Park in a month.

Then Paul thought of his friend Tom. Tom, a city kid, had attended a Christian high school in Lustre, Montana, and lived to tell about it. In fact, he spoke highly of the school: it was a good experience for him.

Paul added it up. A good education. A good Bible teacher—Paul knew his reputation, and approved. A new environment—country life—would be a major change of pace for Tito. Out in the middle of nowhere, Lustre offered no trouble for Tito to get into. No gangs. No bars. No drugs. Sure, Tito would have a hard time adjusting to country life, but he wouldn't be able to run back to Chicago on a whim. The cost was not prohibitive. Paul might have to hit up some friends for contributions, but he could get the money to send Tito to Lustre—if Tito wanted to go.

Tito was back in Chicago for a few days in the middle of that summer. Paul took him to dinner and sprang the idea on him. It was not a total surprise for Tito. Paul had been dropping hints as the plan had developed. But here it was, all laid out for him: The money was available, the school would accept him; did Tito want to go?

He was ready. He said yes.

Grandmother was still in Puerto Rico; she might not have liked the idea of her beloved grandson going so far away. But Tito's mom was agreeable. She was worried about both Luis and Tito as they began to dabble in street violence. Montana would be safer than Chicago. Maybe that would be best. Tito didn't tell his dad until shortly before he left.

Camp closed in late August and Tito returned home. It was only a week before he'd hop that train for Montana. He was a bit excited, a bit scared. He walked the streets with a bit more confidence. He still had to keep an eye out for the Latin Disciples, but he was getting out of the city. He watched the children playing the sidewalk games he used to play, and he realized that many of them would spend their whole lives on these streets. Shooting marbles today, they'd be shooting drugs tomorrow, and maybe shooting people after that. Their only ticket out would be a prison sentence in Peoria or St. Charles. Or maybe death. But Tito was getting out of the city. He had his Amtrak ticket stashed safely in his room.

Paul came by that Saturday. They drove up to Fullerton, to a mini-mall of stores. As Paul wheeled his Datsun back into a parking place, he said, "Let's go in here. I've got to buy some things."

They walked into The Gap and started browsing through the shirts. Paul pulled one off the rack and held it up. "What do you think, Tito? Do you like this?"

"It's all right," Tito answered.

"But not great. OK, how about this? Do you like this better?"

"Yes," Tito answered. "That's a lot nicer."

Paul put the first shirt back and draped the other over his arm as they went to the next rack. He held up another. "How do you like this? A bit gaudy, don't you think?"

"You'd never catch *me* wearing it," Tito teased, "but for an old guy like you . . ."

Paul put it back and chose another. He had a silly smile on his face. Tito had never shopped for clothes with him before: maybe Paul just got a kick out of new shirts.

The day went on like that. Shirts, sweaters, a few pairs of jeans. Paul solicited Tito's opinion on everything and piled up the selections on Tito's waiting arms. The cashier stuffed the goods into bags as Paul shelled out several crisp fifty-dollar bills.

"What, did you rob a bank or something?" Tito gibed.

Paul grinned. "No, Tito. This is honest money. I

know you probably haven't seen a lot of this in your life, but this is hard-earned cash."

They went over to Thom McAn for some shoes. They went back and forth along the shelves, evaluating the various styles. Tito was eyeing the running shoes.

A salesman came by. Paul pointed out the styles he liked. "What size?" the man asked.

"Ten, I think," said Paul.

"Have a seat, then. I'll be right out."

Paul grabbed Tito and they both sat down, awaiting the salesman's return.

"I still don't get this," Tito said. "Did they make you president of the transit authority? Is that why you need all these new clothes?"

"No," Paul said, smiling. "But I am thinking about running for mayor."

The man came out with several boxes of shoes. He knelt in front of them.

"Take off your shoes, Tito," said Paul.

"What?"

"Take off your shoes! Size ten, is that about right?"

As a bewildered Tito complied, Paul told the salesman, "They're for him."

Tito had never had two pairs of dress shoes before. He had never owned running shoes, just cheap sneakers. As the salesman offered the shoes, he slid his feet inside. Still dazed, he stood and tested them out.

"How do they feel?" the man asked.

Tito turned to Paul as the full realization struck him. "Do you mean that all of this is for me. The shirts, the sweaters, the jeans?"

Paul had that silly smile again. He nodded.

"Do they fit all right?" the man repeated.

"Yeah," Tito answered. "They fit fine."

In the car Tito totaled up the cost of the merchandise. It came to more than five hundred dollars.

"Five hundred dollars!" he gasped. "How can you do this for me?"

"When you're out in Montana, I don't want you looking like some inner-city kid. They dress differently out there. I want you to fit in."

"But five hundred dollars! Paul!"

"It's not my money."

"I knew it. You robbed a bank."

"No, Tito," Paul laughed. "It's God's money. He gave me the energy to earn it. It belongs to him. He just lets me use it for important things. And, well, it's important for you to fit in out at Lustre. Someday you'll be able to buy clothes for someone else."

"Yeah, maybe," Tito mumbled. He looked over at the big guy at the steering wheel. Paul's eyes scanned the city streets as he drove, watching for any hint of danger. Days and nights spent operating Chicago buses had taught him to drive carefully, anticipating problems, avoiding them before accidents happened. Tito felt comfortable with Paul at the wheel. Paul was driving him not only through Chicago, but into adulthood, into God's kingdom, out of danger. He would be all right.

"Thank you," he said softly.

Tito wanted to wear everything right away, but Mom had insisted that he pack it away, saving it for Montana. The day finally came when Tito lugged his suitcases out to Paul's car. He threw them in the hatchback and went back to hug his mother good-bye.

Dad went with Paul and Tito on the drive downtown to Union Station. Tito got last-minute advice from both of them. Work hard. Don't get too homesick. Be yourself. Don't worry. Make friends. Don't goof off.

Paul seemed strangely hesitant, as if he were second-guessing his own decision to send Tito out there. "It'll be great," he told Tito. "You'll love it out there." But his eyes belied his words. Paul was afraid it might not work. Tito was going far away, beyond Paul's reach. He would have to make it on his own.

Tito hugged both of them good-bye, his father and his substitute father, and boarded the train to Wolf Point, Montana.

18. Home on the Range

The train ride lasted twenty hours. Tito spent much of it with his nose to the window. He had never seen such scenery. Wheat fields. Farmhouses. Wide open spaces. Blue skies extending forever. Not a skyscraper in sight. Tito was a kid in a candy store. Now this all belonged to him.

Jim Upton met him at the Wolf Point station. Tito wasn't hard to pick out. Everyone else who got off the train was quite white, and Tito's bushy hair came into view well before he did. All alone for a few moments in a brand new world, Tito was glad when a man approached and said, "You must be Tito."

On the forty-minute drive to Lustre, Jim introduced himself. He and his wife, Mary Ann, were dorm parents. Since this was Tito's home away from home, he could feel free to call them Mom and Dad. He could come to them with any problem, but he could also expect to be disciplined by them if he broke the rules.

He explained that Lustre Academy was a good school. There were nearly thirty students attending. About a dozen came from the town of Lustre. The rest came from farther away, though most were from Montana. These lived in the dorm during the school year. The school had certain rules, and the dorm had certain rules, which Tito would eventually learn. There might not be as much excitement in Lustre as Tito expected, but there were lots of good people around. They had fun.

Tito kept looking out the window as the pickup truck sped over a lonely road. It was Sunday morning. The sun, newly risen, was all pink and orange. It sent its soft dawn rays to kiss the fields awake. There was nothing for miles, just fields and fields, telephone poles stretching the wires of civilization between occasional farmhouses. Tito had thought the world was made of concrete.

After nearly a half-hour on one road, Jim steered the van onto a gravel road. "Are we almost there?" Tito asked.

"Not yet," said Jim. Twelve miles later, he pulled in front of the buildings that housed Lustre Academy.

"So this is Lustre," Tito said, unimpressed. He wondered how he would ever learn to live here. Jim helped carry Tito's luggage to his dorm room. Since it was the day before school started, no one was there yet. The building had a fresh smell to it. "Looks like you've got time to take a shower and get dressed," Jim announced. "We'll leave for church in an hour."

Church was strange. It was a Mennonite Brethren church a couple of miles from the school. Tito was all gussied up in the new duds Paul had bought him—sharp new suit and tie. He quietly walked the aisle behind the Uptons and sidled beside them into the pew. He might as well have set off firecrackers. Every eye was on the brown-skinned kid with the huge Afro. Tito felt their stares, heard their whispers. He was the alien here, the extraterrestrial. He really didn't mind so much. At least he was getting attention.

The organ played softly, the choir sang reverently, the pastor preached logically, the people listened attentively. It was all so tame. Tito had never been crazy about his grandmother's Pentecostal church back home, but now he missed the boisterous music, the shouted Amens. Would he ever feel like he belonged here?

On Monday the principal invited Tito to his office. Dan Carden was new to the school himself. Only twenty-seven years old, he had previously served as a missionary in the Bahamas. He wore a mustache and beard in an attempt to look older, but his youthful energy gave him away. He welcomed Tito with a warm smile and offered him a seat. They bantered a bit about the train ride and settling in. Mr. Carden said some of the usual words about the future being bright and full of possibilities—the kind of things people say on the first day of school and at graduations. Tito didn't like all this talk about the future. No one really knows what the future will be, so why talk about it? Why not just get on with it? But Mr. Carden was circling in on something, something he wasn't sure how to say.

"I've been talking with some of the other people here in the community—"

"Talking about me?" Tito interrupted, already pretty comfortable with this easygoing principal.

"Well, yes, as a matter of fact," Mr. Carden continued. "We recognize that you come from a different environment. I myself have spent the last few years in a very needy area in the Bahamas and—well, I know how different things can be, how difficult they can sometimes be."

Tito was nodding, not really agreeing, just trying to hurry him along.

"Tito, we've decided that it would be best for you, and for everyone, if you didn't date while you were here."

So that was it.

"A number of families in this community send their daughters to this school and, well, they don't know quite what to expect from you. They're afraid that you, coming from the inner city, might bring certain influences and, well, they would be a lot more comfortable if you didn't go out with their daughters."

It didn't bother Tito much. He knew he was different. He didn't expect people to be so straightforward about it, but at least they were honest. He'd show them. He had been proving himself all his life, and he'd prove himself here. He would work hard. He would be a star athlete. Those same families would soon be in the stands cheering him on to victory. They'd learn.

"And I think this will turn out well for you, Tito." Mr. Carden was going on, trying to soften the blow. "This will enable you to concentrate on your studies. A lot of students, when they come to a new school, get sidetracked by the social life. You'll be able to get a good start academically."

Tito liked this man, in spite of this restriction he had placed on him. He sensed that Mr. Carden respected him, respected his feelings. He decided to return that respect.

Classes at Lustre challenged Tito. He had won honors at Clemente with little effort; now he had to work. He joined the junior varsity cross-country team. Mr. Carden coached cross-country and urged all the boys to sign up. Tito had never run competitively before, but soon he was winning the junior varsity races consistently.

The varsity and junior varsity teams practiced together on Monday afternoons. A pack of boys would set off together across the open terrain, toward the Mennonite Brethren church, three miles away. But on the way back, Steve, the best runner, would be way ahead of the others, striding confidently, head held high. Tito would follow, a few minutes later, straining with each step to close the gap, and then the line of others, struggling forward, panting and puffing. Mr. Carden stood at the finish line, with stopwatch and clipboard, greeting each runner as he crossed.

In the last practice, however, Mr. Carden looked up to see Tito crossing the line first. "What are you doing here, Tito Mosquito?" he asked. Tito just beamed. He had finally bested the best runner. Steve strode in twenty seconds later, smiling sheepishly. For him it was a small embarrassment in a great career. But Tito prized the moment: he had proven his ability. Yet even this didn't win Tito what he wanted most. He still didn't fit in.

At times he wore his difference like a badge. It was his entree into the society. He was that crazy Puerto Rican from Chicago. Everybody knew him. How did he learn to run so fast? Running away from gangs—so the joke went. It wasn't far from the truth.

Sam Ortmann took Tito horseback riding. After getting Tito saddled up, Sam started off his horse at an easy gait. Tito's horse followed. The city kid knew nothing about stirrups, so he was bouncing around, falling off, legs flailing. He cried, "Help me! Help me! I'm going to die!" Sam laughed, and came back to help.

Tito learned to mock himself, to play the role of the "extraterrestrial." He was always clowning around. He won many friends, but got more than his share of teasing. For weeks he'd hear, "Help me! Help me! I'm going to die!" It wasn't cruel, just funny. He didn't mind being the brunt of that joke. It was a way of being noticed.

For a while Tito was coming up behind people and slapping them hard, very hard, on the back: "Hey, pal, how ya doing?" It was all in fun—or was it? Was he subconsciously telling them that their gibes hurt more than it seemed?

Once, studying in his room, he was summoned to the lounge for a phone call. He went as he was, in his long johns. This was a serious breach of etiquette—it was a coed lounge. Jim Upton called him on the carpet for that one. But Tito shrugged; he was just being the crazy Puerto Rican.

He missed Chicago. There he fit in. In a community of Puerto Ricans, he could be just crazy Tito. He missed Luis, his alter ego. He longed to go striding down the sidewalk shoulder to shoulder with his brother. He missed Paul, and those heart-to-heart talks where everything would suddenly make sense. He missed Richard and Emilio.

Montana looked ugly to him now. Flat, empty. Humboldt Park may have been a bit rundown, but it had character. You walked three blocks and you got somewhere. In Lustre, you walked three blocks and you were still in Lustre. Tito counted the days till Christmas break.

One day Tito was working on the cattle chute with his friend Sam and Sam's dad. He wasn't used to this farm work yet—he was still a city kid at heart—but he was learning. Suddenly he felt a sharp kick in the back of his leg. His instincts, trained through years of city fighting, instantly retaliated. He tightened his fist, tensed his arm, whirled around . . . and punched a young calf square in the nose.

Sam and his father doubled over in laughter. The calf was mildly dazed. Tito sprained his wrist.

Finally, Christmas came, and Tito took the long train ride back home to Chicago, not entirely sure he'd be coming back to Montana. But the vacation wasn't what he expected. All those good times he had been missing as he sat and languished in Big Sky country weren't there anymore. Luis wasn't around much; he had different friends. Of course, Richard and Emilio weren't there either. Tito spent a lot of time with Paul, and that was good, but there really wasn't much of a place for him anymore in Humboldt Park.

He sat around his house on Christmas Day and found himself missing Montana. His family wasn't celebrating Christmas as they used to. Nothing much was happening. He imagined what kind of partying they must be doing at Lustre. His friends were probably gathering around their trees, exchanging presents, singing carols, eating turkey. He wished he could be with them.

When the vacation was over, Tito practically jumped on the train back to Wolf Point. The twenty hours couldn't go fast enough. He longed to see his friends again. He would make a home for himself in Lustre. He would fit in.

Midway through January, Tito lay in his bunk, half-studying, half-mulling over the basketball game he had just lost. Tito never liked to lose, and it seemed that Lustre's junior varsity team would be losing a lot. Tito himself had missed some key shots. Basketball was new to him. "Dad" Upton had spent hours teaching him to dribble, to pull up into a jump shot, to do the pick-and-roll. But after all that practice, Tito still wasn't helping the team much. Maybe basketball just wasn't his game.

A knock at the door. "Hey, Tito, come on down to the lounge. There's someone to see you." He pulled some jeans on over his long johns (he had learned his lesson) and traipsed down to the lounge, wondering who it could be.

He stepped into the lounge and saw dozens of friends and classmates. "Surprise!" they yelled. Someone brought out a cake with sixteen candles as the crowd crooned an out-of-tune "Happy Birthday." Tito was stunned. He finally felt at home.

19. Montana Miracles

Lustre sits in the northeast corner of Montana, one loosely settled farming town among hundreds that dot the Great Plains of Canada and the U.S. About twenty-five miles to the south is the Missouri River, along which Lewis and Clark traveled a century-and-a-half ago. As they explored this region, Captain Lewis noted in his journal that the adjoining country was "level, fertile, open, and exceedingly beautiful." That beauty must have inspired the later settlers who named Lustre, convinced they had found a brilliant gem of territory.

Though the whole area is now part of the Fort Peck Indian Reservation, the current residents of Lustre hail from German stock, descendants of the wave of German immigrants that came in the early 1900s. They carry on the family traditions—wheat farming, raising livestock, going to church.

Tito was getting better at basketball all the time, but midway through the season, he tore a ligament in his leg. Dad Upton drove him to see a chiropractor in town.

The doctor examined Tito and announced that he needed to take it easy for a while. The leg would heal, but it needed rest to heal right.

"How long before I can play basketball again?" Tito wanted to know.

"I'd say about a year," the doctor answered.

Tito's spirits sank. He quietly cried as he sat in the back of the Uptons' van on the ride back to school. He tried to imagine a year of "taking it easy." That ruined not only basketball season, but also track in the spring and cross-country in the fall. He had been making a place for himself here by excelling in athletics. Without that, he'd just be Tito. Not Tito the star—Tito the cripple. He would limp around campus and no one would care.

"Be glad you're not a horse," Dad Upton piped up from the driver's seat in an effort to rescue Tito from his reverie. "When they break a leg, we shoot 'em."

Tito smiled in self-pity. *You might as well shoot me*, he thought. *If I can't run, there's not much for me to do here*.

"Tito?" Dad asked, suddenly serious. "How great do you think God is?"

"What do you mean?" a bewildered Tito responded.

"Could God heal your leg?"

Tito considered his dorm dad's proposition. He

had never really considered that. Prayer like that was a part of his grandmother's world, not his own. For him, when bad things happened, you took your lumps, you bore the pain, you played it tough. Why should God make things easier for you?

But God had helped him, time and time again, bringing Paul to him after Richard died, protecting him from the Latin Disciples, giving him a home here in Montana. But this was different. Why would God care about a basketball injury?

"I guess he could," Tito answered. He was still puzzled by the idea. Sure God could heal him, but would he overrule the doctor in this case? Was Tito's basketball season all that important to the God of the Universe?

"Don't worry, Tito," Dad Upton assured him. "We'll pray for you when we get home."

Back at the dorm, in the Uptons' apartment, Jim and Mary Ann prayed together with Tito that God would heal his leg—if it was his will. A week later Tito was playing basketball again. His leg was fine.

This made an impression on Tito. As he turned it around in his head, he tried to explain it away. Maybe the injury was not that serious to begin with. Maybe the chiropractor was wrong. But he kept coming back to the simple, calm faith of the Uptons. "God will take care of you," they had said, until it finally began to sink in. God could heal Tito's leg, if he wanted, or he could help Tito deal with the injury, which might have been a greater miracle. Either way, God cared. There are few greater truths for a young man, forging a new life in the wilderness, to grasp. God cared for Tito.

As his faith grew that second semester, so did Tito's confidence. He had always seemed sure of himself, but that was just a front. He desperately wanted to be liked and admired; the cockiness was protection against the hurt of rejection. But now he was relaxing more. God loved him and was showing his love through people like Jim and Mary Ann Upton. Another Christian couple, Richard and Lois Korns, also helped support Tito in this adjustment process. Richard pastored the Evangelical Mennonite Brethren Church in Lustre. He and Lois often opened their home to Tito, inviting him to dinner and offering valuable advice.

With this support, and the growing acceptance of the other students, Tito could begin to love himself. He could develop honest relationships now that he was talking and listening, not just posing.

When he learned that his church had an Awana program, Tito was ecstatic. He became coach of its Olympic team, doing everything just as Paul had done. He worked those kids to death and praised them to death. At the regional Olympics the team walked in carrying their sneakers and sat down in unison. Tito adopted the same strategies and expected the team to win every event. They won all but two.

Tito studied hard that spring, improving his grades. He also ran on the track team, nearly making it to the state finals. And he even began to date some of the Lustre Academy girls. No one seemed to mind. In these high school years his girlfriends helped smooth his rough edges. They eased him away from some of his inner city thinking.

Buck Rogers no longer filled Tito's daydreams. Now he imagined himself as Louis L'Amour's hero, Tell Sackett, cool and courageous in the Wild West. He was actually growing to like this country. It was a land for the individualist. The city was a group place—gangs, families, teams. But out here it was every man for himself. Not that people didn't help each other; they did. Tito had never known such great hospitality. But each individual had a value all his own.

In the city, you see a guy's color, his clothes, his walk, and you know where he lives, what he does, what gang he's in—everything you need to know about him. In Montana you have to get to know each person.

This individualism broke down with race relations. After a century-and-a-half of conflict with the Indians, the white folks of Lustre were used to viewing nonwhites with suspicion. At school Tito won people over. Soon they didn't care about his brown skin. Dan Carden had also brought some black Bahamians to the school. Their classmates enjoyed them. But there was still resistance from some of the townspeople. Tito sensed it on his trips into Wolf Point, and in some of the games with other schools in the area. He was an oddity.

Tito had to get used to the fact that he would draw

attention. Walking down the street, he would get stares from people. This part of Montana just didn't have many people of his color. Even at school, lighthearted joking sometimes turned to racial name-calling. In basketball games Tito would get shoved unnecessarily. Usually he shoved back. His temper fulfilled the expectations of those who tried to pick on this "hot-blooded Latin." He seldom backed down from a challenge.

Tito and his black friends from the Bahamas were, by their very presence, expanding the world of some of their classmates, and their families, and the whole town. Not that the town was full of ruthless bigots; these were generally good Christian people. But some didn't know how to deal with a Puerto Rican like Tito. Some just gawked, others acted in more negative ways. Over the course of Tito's stay in Lustre the people were learning to accept and value those of other races. And Tito was learning that he could not fight his way into this community. He would earn his place through love and hard work.

20. Commencement Activities

Thanks in part to Dan Carden's marketing ability, Lustre Academy had grown to forty students by Tito's senior year. The "crazy Puerto Rican" had become a fixture at the school. He had won not only notoriety but popularity as well. People didn't just know him, they liked him. Tito continued to excel in sports and in his studies, and he had coached the church's Awana team to three straight titles.

As graduation day approached, Tito began to feel some jitters. Montana had turned into Paradise for him, but soon he would have to leave. Where would he go? Back to Chicago, where else? But what was left there for him? His family. Yes, it would be great to be with them again, but he had changed and so, surely, had they. Luis, he knew, was running with gangs now. Tito loved his brother dearly, but it would be tough to pal around with him again. Paul was back in Chicago, and Tito looked forward to renewing that friendship. But how long would Paul be there for him? Paul had given and given and given to Tito, but eventually he would have to get on with his own life. And Tito would have to tackle Chicago alone.

In his letters, Paul had been urging Tito to apply to his old school, Moody Bible Institute. Just a few miles from Humboldt Park, Moody was renowned for its Christian training. Whatever God was making of Tito, he could surely use Moody to do it.

Tito had to admit it made sense. Moody was tuition-free, and he'd be in Chicago, not far from his family. But there was something bothering him about going back to Chicago. Would he be able to survive on those old streets? He had noticed on vacations in the city that his reflexes had dulled a bit. Walking down the street, he was a bit more complacent—not so ready to run or defend himself at a moment's notice. Lustre's easy pace had taken the edge off Tito's street smarts. It might take a while to get that back. And for all he knew the Latin Disciples might still be after him. Certainly with Luis hanging out with a gang these days, it was possible that Tito would get drawn into a fray. Those slow reflexes could get him killed.

Not that he was afraid. He just didn't want to go back to his old life. A butterfly is naturally reluctant to crawl back into the caterpillar's cocoon. Part of him wanted to say, "Bring on those Latin Disciples!" But Tito had become a disciple of Jesus. He had learned so many phenomenal things in Montana about himself, about people, about God. Would this knowledge work back home in Chicago? Could he ever function again back on his old turf?

Graduation weekend involved an awards ceremony on Friday night and a commencement service Sunday. To Tito's surprise, his father, grandmother, and both brothers came out from Chicago. Paul also took the long train ride to Montana; he was the commencement speaker.

Tito sat with his brothers during the awards ceremony. Various coaches and teachers took the stage and spoke glowing words about their students. They called names of those receiving awards, and these students trotted up on stage to claim them. Tito got plenty of exercise that night. His brothers would push him out of his seat when his name was called and they'd cheer loudly as he accepted his prizes.

The most precious award Tito received was his induction into the National Honor Society. The folks back home had considered him stupid. Even his family doubted what he could accomplish. But here he had proved his abilities. A Puerto Rican kid from a barrio of Chicago had come to a white, middle-class environment and succeeded. Tito was bursting with pride. So were his brothers.

On Saturday Tito invited his friends and their

families to the school for a feast prepared by his grandmother. She was a bit nervous—she wasn't in her own kitchen—but she graciously whipped up dinner for over thirty people.

Later Tito was playing some basketball with his brothers, just horsing around, one-on-one—on one. It had been quite a while since all three Matias boys had played together like this. The boys, now young men, threw all their machismo into the game—boxing out for the rebound, reaching in for the steal, going up to block a shot, even taunting their opponent when they beat him for a lay-up. At one point Tito got an elbow swung into his face. The action stopped for a moment as Tito hunched over, holding his eye. But when he could see clearly again, play resumed.

The next morning he had a huge black eye.

"You can't go to graduation like that," said his girlfriend, Lois.

"Why not?"

"You'll look awful!" she explained. "Here, let me put some makeup on it."

Tito protested. "I'm not going to wear any makeup."

"Come on," Lois insisted. "Just to cover up your black eye. No one will notice."

So Tito wore makeup to the graduation ceremony. But he didn't wear socks. That had become a trademark of his at Lustre. He would regularly go to classes with his bare feet stuffed into his shoes. The sockless wonder was not about to break his tradition, although his grandmother urged him to reconsider.

The school gym was packed for the ceremony. Relatives and friends from Lustre and throughout Montana had come to witness the event. Tito lined up with his classmates outside, ready to file in. Wearing the mortarboard hat and the gown, which hung down nearly to his bare ankles, he was joking around as usual. The doors opened and the grads filed in.

Tito took a look at the crowded gym and felt the urge to cry. He wasn't sure why. Was it happiness or sadness? Was he proud of his accomplishments or sorry it would all be ending soon? This was a very important moment in his life. Who would have thought that he would make it here?

He caught the eye of his father, and in that moment he saw more love from him than he ever had before. The tough, self-assured man whom Tito had grown up loving and hating, avoiding and longing for, was now fighting back tears. Tito looked down the row at Ricky, the older brother he had idolized, and Luis, the kid brother he had shared his childhood with. "Look at me now," he seemed to say to them, with a smirk and a swag of his head.

And then Tito saw his grandmother, the woman who had poured her lifeblood into his upbringing. She had prayed for him every night. Here her prayers were answered. Tito loved her so very much. He had not always been able to show her that he appreciated her long-suffering, her prayers, even her discipline. He felt that love welling up inside of him, and suddenly the dam burst. Tears streamed from his eyes, over the makeup and down his cheeks.

After preliminary comments from various school and town officials, Paul got up to speak. It was a proud moment for him, and he said so. Tito was like a son to him, so he felt he could relate to the parents in the audience.

Tito was still crying when the time came for the graduates to exchange cards and gifts. They lined up again, and then, one by one, they ran the gauntlet, greeting each friend and offering their remembrance. When his turn came, Tito looked each friend in the eye and thanked him or her for being a friend. His bruised eye was shiny black by now, with rivulets of brown makeup running down his face. It gave them something to laugh about. "You know me," Tito joked. "Anything to get attention." His mind raced back to the early days at school when his whole identity depended on getting that attention, making a name for himself. He had cried himself to sleep some nights because he wasn't sure how he could win the acceptance of his classmates. Now his classmates were hugging him, shaking his hand, offering their good-byes. "Keep in touch," someone said. "Let us know how you're doing."

"So," remarked another. "I guess it's back to Chicago for you."

Tito's heart jumped as he was forced to think

about an uncertain future. "I guess so," he answered.

The plan was for Tito to stay in Lustre for another week to finish up some business, then to go back to Chicago. He'd enroll at Moody in the fall.

But after a week, Tito wasn't ready to go home. He needed more time. Chicago still scared him, and he didn't want to say good-bye to Montana just yet. He had the train ticket to Minneapolis, the plane ticket from there to Chicago, but at the last minute he decided to cancel the trip. When Paul went to meet the plane at Midway Airport, there was no Tito. In a hurried, worried call to Lustre, Paul learned of Tito's change of plans.

"Sorry, Paul," Tito explained. "I guess I just got cold feet."

"That's what you get for not wearing socks."

"Listen, Paul. I just need more time here. Another week. Is that OK?"

"Sure, Tito. I understand. But let me know when you're coming in."

Tito got a job working on a farm near Lustre. It was hard work, but satisfying. The aches in his muscles at day's end told him he was earning his keep. He began to think that maybe he could live out here, full-time, work the land, raise a family. He wrote to Paul, telling him he wouldn't be coming home just yet. Maybe another week or so.

"Are you coming home or what?" Paul asked on the phone a week later. He didn't sound happy.

"Yeah, I am," said Tito. "I'm just not ready yet."

"Why aren't you ready? What are you waiting for?"

Tito thought a moment. "I . . . I don't know. I just don't feel right about it."

"You're scared, aren't you?" Paul challenged.

"No way!"

"You're afraid that you can't make it in the city anymore, aren't you?"

Paul had, as usual, hit the nail on the head. Tito hated to admit he was right. "Well . . ."

"Tito, how great do you think God is?"

"What?"

"Listen to me." Paul had that preacherly tone about him. "God took care of you in Montana, right? He can take care of you in Chicago. Look, Tito, there's a Bible verse, Joshua 23:14. Do you know that one?"

"Not off the top of my head."

"It says, 'Not one thing has failed of all the good things which the Lord your God spoke concerning you.' That's your story, Tito. Don't you see? God is doing something with you, he's been doing it all along. 'Not one thing has failed.' He has kept all his promises. Now, I don't know exactly what God has in store for you, Tito. But I don't think he's been preparing you to be a farmer in Montana. You may think that, but I don't. I think he wants you back in the city. He's been using Montana to bring you back to the city. He hasn't been using the city to send you to Montana. I'm sorry if I've said too much, Tito, but I thought you needed to hear it. Think about it."

The next week, a full month after graduation, Tito boarded the train for Chicago.

21. When God Calls

On a Sunday morning in the winter of 1873, Dwight L. Moody walked on the Clark Street Bridge over the Chicago River toward his tabernacle. Once a shoe salesman, he had been called to the gospel ministry. By now he had gained worldwide fame as an evangelist.

A woman joined Moody on this wintry walk. She was Emma Dryer, the former principal of Illinois State Normal University. She had first met Moody through mutual friends in 1870. When the Chicago Fire struck in 1871, she left the school to assist in Moody's relief efforts.

But as the wind whipped their clothes about them on this particular morning, Moody's thoughts turned to education. He wanted to start a school for girls, to train them in Christian thought and ministry. He had friends among the business moguls of the city who would gladly donate funds for such an enterprise. Dryer would give the school the academic clout it needed.

She thought about the preacher's proposition as they walked together. It should be coeducational, she said. Men need Christian training as well as women. Moody didn't want to compete with the seminaries. A number of schools were training men for ministry; he wanted his school to be unique.

They agreed to disagree for the moment. Moody was off to England for an extended evangelistic campaign. They would explore this idea further when he returned.

But other ideas crowded Moody's schedule for several years. When he finally began planning his training institute in the late 1870s, he had changed his tune about the seminaries. They just weren't doing the job.

Often, he said, a student "comes out of a theological seminary knowing nothing about human nature; he doesn't know how to rub up to these men and adapt himself to them and then gets up a sermon on metaphysical subjects miles above these people. We don't get down to them at all. They move in another world."

The desire to reach people on their level spawned a short-term Bible institute. Professor W. G. Moorehead of Xenia University in Ohio came to teach the Bible in a month-long series of classes in May 1882. Moody challenged the Chicago Evangelistic Society to raise $250,000 to expand these classes into a regular training school, to purchase a building and endow a professorial chair. The society came through.

The school eventually took the name Moody Bible Institute.

About a hundred years later, Tito Matias was accepted as a student there. It had not been a good summer for Tito. Just one week back from Montana, he called Phantom Ranch camp. "Do you need me? I'll be there." He didn't want to stay in Humboldt Park.

At camp he kept turning the future around in his head, like a kaleidoscope, seeing a different picture with each turn. What would Moody be like? Would he make it in the city? And what about after Moody? What did God have in mind for him? What were these "promises" Paul had mentioned? What was God doing?

Tito felt very alone. The camp was full of loving friends, but no one knew his struggle. Paul had moved to South Holland, Illinois, to become youth pastor at a church there. It was just the other side of Chicago, but it might as well have been Europe. Paul was pulling out of his life; Tito knew it. Paul had done his job. Thanks to Paul meeting with Tito, studying the Bible, and praying with him, Tito had grown in his faith. Paul had gotten him through Lustre and into Moody. Now it was all up to Tito. If Paul hung around, he'd be a crutch. Tito would never learn to walk by himself. But these first few steps were so hard.

By working in maintenance at Moody, Tito was able to pay room and board; he didn't have to live in Humboldt Park. He also received some assistance from Inner City Impact. This was a relief for him. He still feared that Lustre had softened him to the harsh realities of inner-city life. All summer he had dreaded the commute between home and school. Now he'd be safe in the dorm. At registration, as he declared his major, he chose Pastoral Studies/Christian Education. With this kind of education, he could go on to a comfortable middle-class life as a pastor or assistant pastor out in the suburbs. He could say goodbye to the city forever.

Later that week Tito sat in the Torrey-Gray Auditorium for the daily chapel service. The massive hall could hold two thousand people; the students filled about half of it. The high wall behind the platform was lined with organ pipes. On certain hymns, the majestic instrument could shake the room. The school president sat on one of several thronelike chairs on the platform, and a speaker, a teacher at the institute, stood at the pulpit, speaking clearly and emphatically.

He was saying normal start-of-the-semester stuff. "You're making decisions now that will affect you all your life." At first it seemed like so much blah-blah-blah, but then it started to make sense. These *were* important decisions.

The speaker continued. "If God is directing you this morning, listen to him. If God is calling you to a certain ministry, go with him. If you are his disciple, you must follow."

The words pounded their way into Tito's brain. Yes, God was directing him. God was calling. But what exactly was he saying?

Tito had no classes immediately after chapel, so he stayed in the auditorium and pondered the message. The other students cleared out, and Tito sat virtually alone in the huge room.

If only those organ pipes could ring out a clear message from God.

I'll go where you want me to go, dear Lord. Just don't make me work in the city.

I've done my time in the city, Lord. It's no fun. It's hard. Friends die. They get arrested. You have to fight all the time. Temptation is everywhere. I'll fall if I go back to the city, Lord. You wouldn't want me to fall away from you, would you?

"Not one thing has failed of all the Lord your God has promised concerning you." *All right. I'll buy that. But what are you promising me. Protection? Strength against temptation?*

Paul seemed so sure that you wanted me in the city, but how could he know? And look at him. He's off to a cushy job in South Holland. Why can't I do that?

"Fear not, for I am with you. Do not be dismayed. I am your God. I will strengthen you; I will help you; I will uphold you with my victorious right hand."

You really want this, don't you, Lord? What choice do I have? I guess I could be a Jonah, huh? Run away and become a fish dinner. Yeah, I guess even a cushy job, if it's not what you want, wouldn't be so much fun. Why is this so hard, Lord?

I'm going to get killed. You know that, Lord. I've got so much Montana in me, I'll get jumped before I can even turn around. But hey, it's your game. You gave me this life, I sort of owe you one.

I'm your disciple. I have to follow you.

Tito changed his major that day to American Intercultural Ministries. He decided he'd serve God in the city.

22. Tito's Epilogue

As a student at Moody, Tito joined a tutoring program. Each Tuesday night he would go to the Montgomery Ward offices and help a little boy from the Cabrini-Green housing project with his homework.

His classes were teaching him to prize the various cultures represented in the city. He began to explore his Puerto Rican heritage as well. He was learning how to express Christian truth in other cultural settings. John 3:16 may mean nothing to the black Muslim gang leader or to the Chinese woman at the pharmacy, but they can see God at work in a Christian's life. Love in action can be far more persuasive than clever words.

Tito worked on the night crew at Moody, mopping floors after classes were over. It was a humbling job for Tito. At first he hated this servile role. He knew he was the equal of anyone in that building. Why should he have to serve them?

Once a month there would be a "Friday Night Sing" at the school, and people from all over Chicagoland would come downtown to enjoy the music. Tito would spend the evening at his job, sweeping up in the halls and offices. Occasionally on these evenings professors or administrators would bring guests through to see their offices. Tito would keep sweeping. He was invisible, just doing his job. This wasn't easy for him. Part of him wanted to walk up to these people and announce, "Look, I'm not just a janitor. I'm just as good as you are. Don't think just because you have fancy clothes and a nice house in the suburbs that you can ignore me!" Yes, Tito had a chip on his shoulder, but that eventually dissolved. Just as he had in Lustre, Tito proved himself at Moody. As he became more secure in his own personhood, he could more willingly serve others.

One day Tito was walking through the neighborhood with his girlfriend, his aunt, and his cousin. They were going to the grocery store. A guy rode by on a bike.

"Hey, aren't you Spike's brother?" "Spike" was Luis's gang name.

"Yeah," Tito answered. "What about it?"

"Well, you better watch your back," the kid said. "You look a lot like him."

Tito recognized this guy. He had been thrown out of Luis's gang and held Luis responsible for that.

Beware of guys with grudges, Tito thought, but he kept walking. The kid rode away.

A few minutes later two cars pulled up beside Tito and his three companions. Ten guys climbed out and stood on the sidewalk, holding bats. At the front was the guy who had been taunting Tito minutes earlier. These were members of the Latin Kings, the guy's new gang. They launched their challenges.

"So you're Spike's brother, huh?"

"Are you as tough as he is—as he *thinks* he is?"

"Your brother put me in the hospital. I ought to do the same to you."

This was the moment Tito had dreaded back when he was pitching hay in Montana. Would he be ready when the city challenged him? God had brought him back here—would he get Tito out of this jam?

Before Tito could respond, his aunt was yelling back at the guys in Spanish. How dare they accost people like this on city streets! They should go home and leave innocent people alone! The gang just laughed at her, making her all the more furious.

Tito broke in. "Hey, I don't know what Spike has or hasn't done to you. I don't care. Gangs aren't a part of my life anymore, OK? I don't have anything to do with it. I'm a Christian now, and as I see it, Christianity and gangs don't mix."

He remembered that he was wearing a Christian T-shirt. "Look, my shirt says, 'Give your heart to Jesus,' and that's what I've done. When I gave him my heart, I had to give up all the hate and violence and everything that was there. Now if you try to take me down, I'll fight back. And God might just give me the power to take you and you and you down with me. I'm not afraid of you, because of Jesus."

His girlfriend was at his shoulder, whispering, "Tito, don't talk too much. There are too many of them." But he was on a roll. He went on, fearlessly, defending himself, talking about Jesus, putting down gang life. He looked sternly down the row of faces as he spoke. The gang stood there, their fingers on their weapons, twitching with nervous energy. Tito stopped talking and waited for their move.

"Let's go," said the guy in front, moving back to one car. They all piled in and the two cars sped away.

The next year Tito got an internship with Inner City Impact. He helped lead the newly formed club in Logan Square and earned academic credits for it.

Joe was his special case. A twelve-year-old Puerto Rican boy, Joe was full of energy. He needed lots of attention. One evening Tito was helping him with his homework.

"Now try this problem, Joe."

"I can't."

Tito laughed. "What do you mean you can't? You haven't tried it yet."

"I just can't do problems like that."

"Look, Joe. You did this problem already, and you were great. You got a little help from me on this one, but you did this one all by yourself. You only have five more to go. You can do it."

"I can't. I'm tired."

Tito stared at the young student. "I don't buy it," he said.

Joe closed the book with a slam. He stood up and threw the book on the floor. "I can't do it!" he exclaimed. He grabbed the papers on the table and threw them down too. "I can't!"

There was no one else in the room, just Tito and Joe facing off. There was an administrator in an adjacent office, but he was apparently letting Tito handle this outburst. Joe picked up his chair and tossed it behind him. "Don't make me do it! I can't! I can't! I can't!"

He stood there, tensed, ready for a fight.

Tito held back a smile. He couldn't help thinking that Joe was another Tito. Clamoring for attention, angry at the world for no good reason, what monsters lurked in his soul? What could Tito do for him?

The old Tito would have yelled at the kid. Obviously Joe wasn't appreciating all the effort Tito was putting into this. Tito could have grown angry. He could have grabbed Joe and pinned him to the floor until he apologized. But the new Tito knew that Joe's needs ran deep. He needed love. The kind of love Paul had shown to Tito.

"Are you finished?" Tito asked calmly.

Joe wasn't quite sure how to handle this response. He was all tensed up with no one to fight.

"Pick up the chair," Tito instructed. Numbly, Joe did as he was told. "Now pick up the book and these papers and let's get back to work."

After three years at Moody, Tito graduated. This was another proud moment for Tito's family, for Paul, for Bill Dillon of ICI. Tito was being launched into a life of Christian service. How many others, like young Joe, would be touched by his ministry?

In the fall of 1987 Tito went on to Greenville College, in southern Illinois, to get a degree in education. At this writing, he plans to do his student teaching in Montana, and return to Humboldt Park to teach history at Roberto Clemente High School.

23. When a Culture Consumes Its Young

Many of Tito's classmates from Moody, and some from Greenville, are headed for the mission field. In a way Tito is, too.

U.S. Secretary of Education William Bennett called Chicago's school system the worst in the nation. "You have close to an educational meltdown," he has said. The *Chicago Tribune* has accused school administrators of "institutionalized child neglect." Student absenteeism runs 11 percent on average, and city-wide the drop-out rate is nearly 50 percent. Reading levels are well below average.

Riddled with gang problems and beset with an alarming dropout rate, Clemente High School is one of the neediest schools within this blighted school system. It offers little help and little hope to the young people of Humboldt Park.

Hope is hard to come by in this part of Chicago.

Gangs emerge, supposedly to give people some power, some control over their own lives, but they perpetuate a cycle of violence that leaves everyone cowering in terror. The community feeds on itself, and the very young people who should be bringing vitality and hope are being ruined in the process.

You don't have to look very far to see the needs. A collection of clippings from the *Chicago Tribune*, summarized here, chronicle the sad state of affairs.

WILLIE

Fifteen-year-old Willie sat in juvenile jail at St. Charles, Illinois. Armed robbery.

Thirty miles east, back in Humboldt Park, Willie's older brother was sitting on a stoop drinking beer with his best friend. A rival gang member shot him eight times.

Willie idolized his brother. As a kid, he had tried to be just like him. When he was nine, still following in his brother's footsteps, he had joined the gang. Over the next seven years, Willie had been arrested thirty times. Most of the charges never reached court. Prosecution wasn't worth the effort: kids seldom get jail. At age twelve he began using the nickname "Will Kill." In seventh grade he dropped out. Then at age fifteen he was snagged for armed robbery. A serious crime, a tough judge—he got eight months at St. Charles.

When Willie heard of his brother's death, he craved revenge. Soon afterward, he was paroled and returned to the city. Two months after that, one September evening, he grabbed his chrome revolver and pedaled his bicycle to enemy turf, the 2900 block of Wabansia. He saw someone who looked like he might be from the local gang.

"I didn't even know the guy's name," he explained later. "I just wanted revenge deeply. But he had the colors, he had on gym shoes, he was showing the symbols, and he was in their territory."

Willie aimed for his heart. He missed, hitting the spinal cord instead, paralyzing him from the waist down.

The guy's name was Tony. He was fourteen.

Four years later, from the maximum-security prison in Joliet, Willie told a reporter, "I could have avoided this if someone had really stuck with me. I thought everyone lived the way I did. They didn't teach me it was wrong. They didn't teach me not to do it again. They didn't give a damn about me. They just locked me up."

Willie also has a younger brother in Joliet, imprisoned for unlawful use of a weapon. Willie has urged him to stay out of trouble when he gets out on parole. But Willie doesn't expect the best. "He hasn't had the time to think like I have. He's just going to fall back into the whole mess."

JAIME

Jaime was thirteen when an undercover cop booked him for selling cocaine. A few months later he was out dealing again on the streets of East Humboldt Park. "He's probably got a couple of eleven- or twelve-year-olds who run drugs for him," says one police officer. "He pays them a dollar or two a bag. When he finally goes to jail, they'll take his place."

Jaime may not go to jail for a while yet. Kids don't get convicted, and the gangs know it. That's why they use youngsters like Jaime—and he uses kids younger than himself—to run drugs. Jaime had been arrested twelve times previously. Only two of those arrests—for burglary and robbery—even made it to court. A *Chicago Tribune* study found that only 1 percent of 1985 juvenile drug arrests in Chicago resulted in convictions.

So Jaime's on the street until he's seventeen. Then, if he's smart, he'll get the younger ones to do the dangerous work for him. That's the way it works with gangs these days.

"We are just arresting the symptoms of a social disease," says the head of Chicago's gang crimes unit. "If a kid drops out of school and can't get a job, who's there for him? The gang. They take him in. He is successful within that sphere, and he can make a good living off drugs."

GEORGE

George Crume was a big, quiet sixteen-year-old. He was a good kid, not involved in gangs. The assistant principal at Clemente High School, where George was a junior, spoke highly of him: "George Crume never was in any trouble. There were no discipline problems whatsoever."

The boy stood in front of a clothing store on Milwaukee Avenue one May evening. According to a witness, a car drove by with five young men inside. A window on the passenger side was rolled down and a shot was fired. The bullet struck George Crume in the right side of his abdomen. Somebody dragged his body to a vacant lot, where he died. Police think the killers mistook George for a rival gang member.

The next morning George's mother wept at the scene of the shooting. Pointing to the patch of red on the sidewalk, she cried out, "That's my baby's blood!"

George's older brother Clay had joined the army and moved away. "I wanted George to be in the army, too," Mrs. Crume told a reporter. "I tried to sign him up, but they said they couldn't take him until he's seventeen. And now . . ."

LEONARD

Sixteen-year-old Leonard Santiago was playing softball in a schoolyard one May evening when a fourteen-year-old rode up to him and started taunting him, calling him names. The kid thought Leonard was an enemy gang member.

It wasn't true. Leonard was a good kid, a sophomore at Clemente High. He had lived for a while in the Bronx and had attended a private boarding school in New Jersey. About a year earlier, he had returned to Chicago to live with his aunt, who had strict rules. "You have to tell us where you're going and you have to tell us when you're coming back," the aunt would tell Leonard and his brother Gus, seventeen. "They didn't like it at first," their aunt said later, "but they listened. Mainly, they stayed on the block."

Gus was with his brother when the fourteen-year-old rode up to them, launched his taunts, and rode away. He had a feeling the kid would be back, so they moved over to the basketball courts—not far enough, as it turned out.

"When we were over at the courts," Gus said later, "the kid came over and took out a piece." The kid shot Leonard Santiago in the abdomen and in the head, killing him.

Now Gus is thinking of joining a gang—for revenge. "I would do what they did," he says.

ANNA

Anna had to display her Clemente High ID card to show "what I really look like." She was a mess, her face swollen, her eyes blackened, her jaw dislocated, her teeth broken, her body bruised. The card showed a pretty, smiling face. "That's me," she said. "I miss myself already."

On two occasions in the previous month, Anna had been asked to join one of the "girl gangs" in Humboldt Park. She had refused.

One April night Anna, sixteen, and her twelve-year-old sister went out to the corner store. It was about eight. A few steps past the padlocked gate that protected their home, Anna was accosted by three girls, twenty-two, sixteen, and thirteen. They berated Anna for wearing a yellow blouse—that was the gang's color—and they gave her one more chance to join their gang. When she said no, they attacked.

"It's hard to believe that such injury could be inflicted by hands and feet," a police officer commented. "She was a beautiful looking girl, but you'd never know it now."

A crowd gathered to watch the beating—about twenty of them. "They didn't help because this neighborhood is made out of gangs," Anna said later. They just looked on as the girls "stomped me like a cockroach."

When Anna's older sister hurried out of the house to help her, the attackers stopped and walked away. Police arrested them two hours later.

"Hopefully they will have to serve time for what they did," Anna said. "I won't be going outside until they do. I'll remain neutral. They will have to kill me before I turn into a gang member."

Police estimated in 1986 that two hundred girls were involved in Humboldt Park gangs.

OLGA

Olga joined a gang in Humboldt Park when she was ten. By age seventeen she was serving her second stint at the juvenile detention center in Warrenville,

Illinois. The first was for intimidation with a deadly weapon. The second was more than intimidation: she led the girls who attacked Anna for not joining their gang. That episode got headlines for Olga—and a return to Warrenville. In her young life Olga has also been convicted for assault, weapons possession, and theft. And she says she has taken "any kind of thing that was drugs."

A few months from possible parole, Olga admitted to a reporter that she didn't expect her life to change. "Once it's in your blood, it's hard to get rid of."

Olga's mother lives in Humboldt Park with most of her eleven children. "Sometimes I feel better that she's in there and off the streets," she says. "If she came home today, she'd probably kill somebody. I honestly don't know if there's hope for her."

The permanence of Olga's plight may be illustrated by the tattoos that cover her arms and back. By her left eye two teardrops are tattooed—"death tears" she calls them, in memory of friends from Humboldt Park who were killed in gang violence.

But in a letter to her mother she writes, "I'm doing fine. Just trying to stay out of trouble and thinking, Why isn't anybody writing me or at least calling me? The question is, Why did everybody give up on me thinking I'm not going to ever change?"

24. The Challenge

Ralph works at Inner City Impact. He used to be "in the trenches," working one-on-one with kids in the neighborhood. Now in his mid-thirties, he has been promoted to a position where he is providing pastoral care for the younger missionary staff that call Inner City Impact their home. But he still has a heart for kids.

There's something of a Clark Kent image that Ralph projects. Mild-mannered, soft-spoken, he has just a touch of an Alabama drawl.

Ralph and his wife live in Humboldt Park, just a few blocks from ICI headquarters. One night at about eleven-thirty he was having his "quiet time," praying and reading the Bible. He was studying the Book of Esther, reading about the young Jewish queen who dared to approach the king and right a wrong. Ralph's wife, eight months pregnant with their first child, had just retired for the night.

Suddenly Ralph heard a commotion outside. He looked out and saw twenty gang members beating up a guy. The poor victim was probably wearing the colors of a rival gang. The gang was surrounding the guy, punching him, kicking him. He would begin to stagger away, and they'd grab him again. Ralph felt he had to stop it.

The gang was already moving away as Ralph ran across the street. The victim was badly bruised, but still alive. Other neighbors were there by now, and already summoning medical help. Ralph felt he needed to confront the gang. He went back inside to put on shoes and a jacket. His wife called to him. "Do you have to go back out there?"

"It's all right, honey. I'll be back."

Ralph walked back across the street and around the corner to where he knew the gang hung out.

They knew who he was. Ralph was a friend of Jimmy, the "prince" of the gang. Years earlier Ralph had befriended Jimmy through ICI activities. So Ralph walked tentatively toward this pack of guys who had just savagely assaulted someone.

"Hey, Ralph," they said. "How's it going?"

Ralph summoned up his courage and told them off. "I asked Jimmy to keep you guys from doing that. I don't want you doing this in front of my house."

When he mentioned Jimmy, they showed immediate respect. "You want to see Jimmy? He's back here." They led him back to their prince, but then a lookout announced that police were coming. The guys rapidly dispersed.

"I have to get out of here," Jimmy said. Ralph invited him home to talk.

They talked until two in the morning—about Jimmy's life, about how hard it was to get out of the gang situation, about Jimmy's secret fears, about God.

"What do you have to be afraid of?" Jimmy charged. "You're perfect."

"That's not true," Ralph answered soberly. "I struggle with a lot of things. I get angry sometimes. I have to deal with lust, with jealousy. I'm far from perfect. But that doesn't matter to God. You don't have to be perfect. You just have to ask for his help. He takes you as you are."

"Yeah, but you don't know the things I've done."

"God knows. And he wants to change you, Jimmy."

Jimmy looked down at his hands, as if they were covered with blood. "It's so hard, man. I don't think I can get out." Ralph saw the two-thousand-dollar gold crucifix Jimmy had bought with drug money. "What am I going to do," he said, "work at McDonald's for minimum wage?"

"God can help you," Ralph persisted. "He can help you start over. And I'll be there if you need me. We can find a job for you. It won't be the big bucks you have now, but what good is all that money if you're living in fear? The Bible says, 'What shall it profit a man if he gains the whole world, but loses his own soul?' That's you, Jimmy."

Jimmy just shook his head. "Who would hire me?"

"I don't know," Ralph stammered. "But you're a bright guy. Somebody would—"

"I can't read, man!" Jimmy blurted out. "They tested me in school. It was, like, second-grade level. Here I was in high school and I was reading 'See Spot run.' That's why I left. It just wasn't worth it."

"I can teach you," Ralph said.

"You would do that for me?"

"After all God has done for me, how could I say no? When do you want to start?"

Jimmy suddenly looked scared. "Let me think about it, man." It seemed like he wanted to go.

"All right, Jimmy. Just let me know. I'm here."

"I know," Jimmy said quietly. There were storms raging inside him. He looked toward the door, then down at the floor.

"Before you go," Ralph said, "I'd like to pray with you. Is that OK? I know you're not quite ready to give your life to God, but I think he's talking to you. Would you mind if I just took a moment here to pray for you?"

Jimmy raised his eyes to Ralph's. "Shoot."

Ralph prayed for Jimmy's guidance and protection, that God would change his life, that God would show Jimmy his power. They said their amens, said their good-byes, and Jimmy strode out into the night.

A few weeks later Jimmy called. He wanted Ralph to teach him to read. They made arrangements to meet a few days later and go to the high school to pick up his records. Ralph needed to know what kind of tutoring Jimmy needed.

On that day Ralph waited for an hour or so. Jimmy didn't show. Ralph figured that Jimmy was just chickening out, as he had before. Later he learned that Jimmy had been arrested—on suspicion of murder.

Ralph is no Superman. He's just a guy who cares. The city needs more people like Ralph, like Paul, like Tito.

Tito's story is played out time and time again in Chicago, New York, L.A., Detroit, Washington, Wilmington, Camden. If you dare to walk down those streets, you'll probably see some ten- or twelve-year-old who's convinced he's worthless—and who will wreak all sorts of destruction in order to prove it. If someone cares enough to show him—not just to tell, but to show by his or her actions—that God loves him, that kid's life could be redeemed.

You get to write the end of that story.

Other Living Books Best-Sellers

ANSWERS by Josh McDowell and Don Stewart. In a question-and-answer format, the authors tackle sixty-five of the most-asked questions about the Bible, God, Jesus Christ, miracles, other religions, and creation. 07-0021-X $4.95.

ANSWERS TO YOUR FAMILY'S FINANCIAL QUESTIONS by Larry Burkett. Questions about credit, saving, taxes, insurance, and more are answered in this handbook that shows how the Bible can guide our financial lives. 07 0025-2 $4.95.

THE BEST OF BIBLE TRIVIA I: KINGS, CRIMINALS, SAINTS, AND SINNERS by J. Stephen Lang. A fascinating book containing over 1,500 questions and answers about the Bible arranged topically in over 50 categories. Taken from the best-selling *Complete Book of Bible Trivia*. 07-0464-9 $3.95.

THE CHILD WITHIN by Mari Hanes. The author shares insights she gained from God's Word during her own pregnancy. She identifies areas of stress, offers concrete data about the birth process, and points to God's sure promises that he will gently lead those that are with young. 07-0219-0 $3.95.

CHRISTIANITY: THE FAITH THAT MAKES SENSE by Dennis McCallum. New and inquiring Christians will find spiritual support in this readable apologetic, which presents a clear, rational defense for Christianity to those unfamiliar with the Bible. 07-0525-4 $3.95.

COME BEFORE WINTER AND SHARE MY HOPE by Charles R. Swindoll. A collection of brief vignettes offering hope and the assurance that adversity and despair are temporary setbacks we can overcome! 07-0477-0 $6.95.

THE COMPLETE GUIDE TO BIBLE VERSIONS by Philip W. Comfort. A guidebook with descriptions of all the English translations and suggestions for their use. Includes the history of biblical writings. 07-1251-X $3.95.

DARE TO DISCIPLINE by James Dobson. A straightforward, plainly written discussion about building and maintaining parent/child relationships based upon love, respect, authority, and ultimate loyalty to God. 07-0522-X $4.95.

Other Living Books Best-Sellers

DR. DOBSON ANSWERS YOUR QUESTIONS by James Dobson. In this convenient reference book, renowned author Dr. James Dobson addresses heartfelt concerns on many topics, including questions on marital relationships, infant care, child discipline, home management, and others. 07-0580-7 $5.95.

400 CREATIVE WAYS TO SAY I LOVE YOU by Alice Chapin. Perhaps the flame of love has almost died in your marriage, or you have a good marriage that just needs a little spark. Here is a book of creative, practical ideas for the woman who wants to show the man in her life that she cares. 07-0919-5 $3.95.

GIVERS, TAKERS, AND OTHER KINDS OF LOVERS by Josh McDowell and Paul Lewis. Bypassing generalities, about love and sex, this book answers the basics: Whatever happened to sexual freedom? Do men respond differently than women? Here are straight answers about God's plan for love and sexuality. 07-1031-2 $3.95.

HINDS' FEET ON HIGH PLACES by Hannah Hurnard. A classic allegory of a journey toward faith that has sold more than a million copies! 07-1429-6 $4.95.

HAVE YOU SEEN CANDACE? by Wilma Derksen. In this inspiring true story, Wilma Derksen recounts the hope and agony of the search for her missing daughter. Through Wilma's faith, readers will discover forgivness and love that overcome evil. 07-0377-4 $5.95.

THE INTIMATE MARRIAGE by R. C. Sproul. The author focuses on biblical patterns of marriage and practical ways to develop intimacy. Discussion questions included at the end of each chapter. 07-1610-8 $3.95.

JOHN, SON OF THUNDER by Ellen Gunderson Traylor. In this saga of adventure, romance, and discovery, travel with John—the disciple whom Jesus loved—down desert paths, through the courts of the Holy City, and to the foot of the cross as he leaves his luxury as a privileged son of Israel for the bitter hardship of his exile on Patmos. 07-1903-4 $5.95.

Other Living Books Best-Sellers

LIFE IS TREMENDOUS! by Charlie "Tremendous" Jones. Believing that enthusiasm makes the difference, Jones shows how anyone can be happy, involved, relevant, productive, healthy, and secure in the midst of a high-pressure, commercialized society. 07-2184-5 $3.95.

LORD, COULD YOU HURRY A LITTLE? by Ruth Harms Calkin. These prayer-poems from the heart of a godly woman trace the inner workings of the heart, following the rhythms of the day and seasons of the year with expectation and love. 07-3816-0 $3.95.

LORD, I KEEP RUNNING BACK TO YOU by Ruth Harms Calkin. In prayer-poems tinged with wonder, joy, humanness, and questioning, the author speaks for all of us who are groping and learning together what it means to be God's child. 07-3819-5 $3.95.

MORE THAN A CARPENTER by Josh McDowell. A hard-hitting book for people who are skeptical about Jesus' deity, his resurrection, and his claim on their lives. 07-4552-3 $3.95.

MOUNTAINS OF SPICES by Hannah Hurnard. Here is an allegory comparing the nine spices mentioned in the Song of Solomon to the nine fruits of the Spirit. A story of the glory of surrender by the author of *Hinds' Feet on High Places*. 07-4611-2 $4.95.

OUT OF THE STORM by Grace Livingston Hill. Gail finds herself afloat on an angry sea, desperately trying to keep an unconscious man from slipping away from her. 07-4778-X $3.95.

QUICK TO LISTEN, SLOW TO SPEAK by Robert E. Fisher. Families are shown how to express love to one another by developing better listening skills, finding ways to disagree without arguing, and using constructive criticism. 07-5111-6 $3.95.

THE SECRET OF LOVING by Josh McDowell. McDowell explores the values and qualities that will help both single and married readers to be the right person for someone else. He offers a fresh perspective for evaluating and improving the reader's love life. 07-5845-5 $4.95.

Other Living Books Best-Sellers

74 MORE FUN AND CHALLENGING BIBLE CROSS-WORDS. This brand-new batch of crosswords features both theme puzzles and general crosswords on a variety of levels, all relating to Bible facts, characters, and terms. 07-0488-6 $3.95.

STRIKE THE ORIGINAL MATCH by Charles Swindoll. Many couples ask: What do you do when the warm, passionate fire that once lit your marriage begins to wane? Here, Chuck Swindoll provides biblical steps for rekindling the fires of romance and building marital intimacy. 07-6445-5 $4.95.

SUCCESS: THE GLENN BLAND METHOD by Glenn Bland. The author shows how to set goals and make plans that really work. His ingredients of success include spiritual, financial, educational, and recreational balances. 07-6689-X $4.95.

WHAT WIVES WISH THEIR HUSBANDS KNEW ABOUT WOMEN by James Dobson. The best-selling author of *Dare to Discipline* and *The Strong-Willed Child* brings us this vital book that speaks to the unique emotional needs and aspirations of today's woman. An immensely practical, interesting guide. 07-7896-0 $4.95.

WINDOW TO MY HEART by Joy Hawkins. A collection of heartfelt poems aptly expressing common emotions and thoughts that single women of any age experience. The author's vital trust in a loving God is evident throughout. 07-7977-0 $3.95.